Praise for **Get Your POWER** *On!*

"For any woman wanting to grow into her personal power, this book is a must. The author has years of personal and professional experience and it shines through in her work. [Get Your Power On! has] practical, realistic, grounded and compassionate advice [for] all areas of life. This is the kind of book any young woman needs and will be helpful for those older as well. Highly recommended."

> - Jeanette Martin, author of *Write Your Book at Fifty: A Call to Women – Discover Your Voice. Open New Doors. Create Your Legacy.*

"Power has been a dirty word for women for a long time. I love how this book reclaims what personal power is all about, and then tells women what it takes to get it in their life. Nancy Jonker shares her own personal experiences, as well as those of women she has worked with, to write a book that is practical, as well as an easy read."

> - Rivka Kawano, author and speaker

"Just what I needed to help me refocus... I especially enjoyed the free workbook download. A perfect tool for anyone looking to embrace their potential!"

> - Holly Wicks

"Approachable and applicable! This book was an easy read with relatable examples for self review, reflection and improvement."

D1453166

Praise for **Get Your POWER** *On!*

"Dr. Jonker has written a very useful and insightful book--one that I plan to use in my own therapy practice, and as a bonus, she has also written a very useful companion workbook. The book itself is an interesting and easy read--chock full of concepts that resonate with anyone who wants to improve their capacity to "own" their personal worth. The workbook extends the usefulness of the book into applicable lessons and opportunities to use the information in highly personal ways. Cheers to you, Dr. Jonker, your readers will feel your spirit and enthusiasm for your subject leap from the book into their own lives!"

> - Dr. Susan Cain, author of *Horse Sense for Leaders: Building Trust-Based Relationships* and co-founder of The Corporate Learning Institute

"I found this book insightful and straightforward. The day after I read it, I was haunted by the chapter on boundaries. Of all the work I have done on myself, I had never looked at boundaries the way Ms. Jonker described it. Something became very clear to me. I could see a pattern in myself that had up until then, remained hidden. I made some real changes in how I relate to women that I had perceived as a threat. It's liberating to not have to operate like that anymore. I have less fear. I've never had the experience of reading a book, seeing something new, knowing what to do, doing it and have a real change happen."

> - Mary Sheehan, RPh, founder of Prescriptions for Happiness

Get Your POWER *On!*

A Woman's Guide to Becoming Confident and Effective in Business, Life, and Relationships

Nancy Jonker, PhD

Get Your Power On! A Women's Guide to Becoming Confident and Effective in Business, Life and Relationships
Copyright © 2016 Nancy Jonker
Published by Dr Nancy Jonker Publishing
www.nancyjonker.com
ISBN: 978-0692702024

Printed in the United States of America

to Bob, Jon and Ben—
for filling me with wonder, life and love;
for challenging me to deepen my personal
power; and for teaching me the art of loving
and letting go

and

to my sisters everywhere—
for sharing with me your stories, your
challenges, and your courage.
It is our shared journey that spurred and
informed the writing of this book.
Now, let's get our power on!

When we do the best we can, we never know what miracle is wrought in our life, or in the life of another.

—Helen Keller

Invitation from the Author

This book is a roadmap for women who want to increase their confidence, expand their competence and create more success at work and at home. *Get Your POWER On!* provides practical strategies to learn the skills you need to get those promotions and raises, be a more effective leader, improve your relationships and enjoy your life more!

Visit
www.NancyJonker.com/GetYourPowerOnIntro
to get my personalized introduction to this book.

This book features bonus material found online.

1. Download a free QR scanner to your phone from unitag.io/app

2. Scan the QR image with your phone

3. View the resources on Nancy's website

4. Let us know if you have any questions by visiting nancyjonker.com or Facebook.com/DrNancyJonker

Contents

Download some FREE tools to help you get started at www.NancyJonker.com/Resources

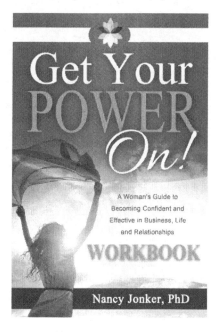

In the **complimentary workbook**, you'll find practices, exercises, and reflective writing prompts compiled in an easy-to-follow format to support you on your journey to a more empowered self.

Also download my **free audio exercises**: Centering Using Visualization and Building the Bridge Between Head and Heart.

Enjoy!

Chapter 1:
What Does Personal Power Look Like?

> *One is not born, but rather becomes, a woman.*
> —Simone de Beauvoir

No one has to think twice about their answer to the question, "Does Oprah have personal power?" Even without defining personal power, it is understood that Oprah possesses it. But when it comes to everyone else, it isn't always so clear. How do you know when you have it? How do you even start thinking about it?

Before anything else, it's useful to consider why anyone would bother worrying about personal power—whether we have it and how to build it. The answer is that when we have it, there is a multitude of benefits that flow to us—much like when we have physical strength, we are able to carry, lift, function, and move effectively and in a balanced way. We are less prone to injury when we're physically strong and can use our muscles in the proper way.

But again, when we have strength without flexibility, we are susceptible to injury. One of the hardest things for trainers and physical fitness instructors to get people to do is to stretch after they exercise! Everyone wants to develop the muscle and burn the fat, but, without continually maintaining and expanding our range of motion, we become limited by the constricted muscles we've worked so hard to develop.

And so it is with personal power—it's a careful balance of mastery and vulnerability. It's tempting to focus on developing strength without the accompanying flexibility and softness. Or maybe for you, it's tempting to resign yourself to living a life without the power and confidence you'd like.

This book is a call to not give in to either of these temptations, but to develop the kind of personal power that includes all of who you are. The world needs powerful leaders who can embrace strength as well as softness. The world needs your powerful self.

Advantages of Personal Power and the Art of Being Fully Yourself

When you have a high level of personal power, you are able to maintain healthy relationships without losing yourself. You have self-respect, which is both a source of personal power and a result of it. With personal power, you are more likely to get paid what you're worth and to have the impact you desire—in your relationships, in your work environment, in your community, and so on. Exercising personal power can shift you from a feeling of depletion to having energy for those people and tasks you love, from overwhelmed to clear, and from rumination to satisfaction.

By now, you should be saying to yourself, "I want more of that!"

As you already know, personal power isn't something you either have or don't have. You possess levels of power on a continuum, and, often, the amount that you have and display is not consistent across all areas of life.

For instance, you may function with a high degree of personal power at work where you have your role and a title to support you but have a much lower level of power at home and in your personal life where different rules seem to apply. When you're with a partner, kids, friends, or people in your community, it can be hard to set personal boundaries and to put your needs on a par with the needs of those you love. Different environmental factors as well as different emotional and connection factors affect how much personal power we have and are willing to exercise in these different arenas.

How a Lack of Personal Power May Look

So let's take a look at what life looks and feels like when we do not have or use personal power. My experience, both in my own life and in working with clients, is that there are telltale signs when we lack personal power.

Feelings of one or more of these: panic, vulnerability, fear, and feeling overwhelmed are relatively constant companions. Effects on our thinking are also signs—effects such as being scattered to the point we can't concentrate, ruminating, and continually worrying.

Lack of personal power shows up in physical ways through exhaustion, playing small, being ineffective, having others ignore us, or not being able to accomplish tasks despite being busy all the time.

Sometimes this lack of personal power shows up in self-doubt that keeps us from taking action. We decide we don't have what it takes and so don't even try. The research actually shows this to be true for a lot of women, as reported in multiple studies in Sheryl Sandberg's *Lean In*. We judge ourselves as less capable than we are and decide not to go after things for which, in reality, we are fully qualified.

Lack of personal power also shows up in relationships when we feel underappreciated, like our voice is not heard or we become resigned because it doesn't pay off to raise conflicts or disagree. We either find ourselves in nitpicky fights that seem unresolvable or we live a life less fully ourselves, so we can accommodate a strong partner.

Sometimes we find ourselves without a relationship because we haven't found a way to be all of who we are and with a significant other at the same time.

The Other Side: A High Degree of Personal Power

In contrast, when you function with a high degree of personal power across the different arenas, you manifest competence in a wide variety of roles, including partner, parent, business person, entrepreneur, manager, or CEO.

You have a sense of empowerment that you bring to virtually every situation you're in, and you derive satisfaction from your efforts. You have efficacy, both internally and in the accomplishment of tasks.

When you have a high degree of personal power, there is an expansiveness about you, and you are willing to take risks. You have the capacity for close, satisfying relationships in which you can be transparent, can bring up conflict, and expect resolution.

When you make a decision as a parent, your children or step-children listen and know it is for real. You have an impact on the world around you, and it does not scare you—in fact, it gratifies you!

If this sounds too good to be true, I get it.

When we're committed to our own growth, we continue to see areas where we can improve and stretch into having and integrating more personal power. When we're constantly working at our edge, we continue to feel the effects of stretching and getting out of our comfort zone.

So, take heart. Feeling the discomfort and aliveness of leaving your comfort zone is a sign you're on the right track—even when it doesn't seem like it.

Carl Jung said, "Where your fear is, there is your task."

My Story

When I was in high school, I remember being awakened to the idea of wanting personal power, except I didn't call it that back then. I decided I wanted to be independent and strong. I didn't know how to accomplish this, so I set about trying to act like I was.

As my life unfolded, I pursued a PhD, married a high-powered man, and made decisions about how to spend my time, so I would appear independent. I did this pretty well and had a number of people fooled.

There were two incidents in my young adult life that brought me up short. Of course, before these happened, I had this nagging sense of unease, a doubt really that I was not the independent woman I presented myself to be. But after these two events happened, I was confident in my need for developing true personal power.

One: Frozen

The first event was during my first year in graduate school. I was in my early twenties and money was tight. I was sharing a one-bedroom apartment in the lower-income part of town with a friend and classmate when our apartment was broken into. It was in the early morning around 5:30 am.

My sleep was interrupted with the sound of loud banging. Like anyone who is trying to sleep, I incorporated the sounds into a dream. I dreamed that the neighbors upstairs were putting furniture together and pounding as they went. It wasn't until my roommate woke up and asked me in an urgent whisper what was going on that I realized there was an intruder in our apartment.

By that time, the intruder had gone from banging the metal cover of the air-conditioning vent back into place to opening and closing cabinet and closet doors. OMG! He was right outside the bedroom door. Next, I saw his gloved hand on the doorknob as he opened the door to the bedroom. My roommate sat bolt upright in bed! And I froze in place.

Fortunately for us, we must have surprised him as much as he surprised us. The black-gloved, male intruder fled our apartment, and we were safe. But not from anything I had done!

What bothered me most about this experience—in addition to feeling violated and intruded upon—was the fact that I froze. It was the most blatant experience I had up to that time which suggested to me I was not a strong, independent woman, but rather a scared woman who, when push came to shove, would freeze in her bed rather than fight or escape.

Two: Paralyzed

The second experience I had was far more subtle but nonetheless powerful. As a young professional, I got called in by the office manager to talk about something I had done. I had recently graduated with my PhD, was working at a local hospital, but didn't know the ins and outs of private practice.

I must have done something to cross her, and she called me in to talk about it. Now, this woman was far less educated than I, she was very short in stature, and she was not, in reality, a powerful or scary person. But she had a very sharp tongue and didn't mind using it. She dressed me down for whatever it was I had done. I don't remember what it was—but I do remember becoming paralyzed—absolutely unable to say anything in my defense. It was like being a kid called into the principal's office!

It was a sad realization for me that having a high degree of education, in psychology no less, did not translate into having more personal power. It didn't translate power into my personal life, but it also didn't help me in the work arena. It hit home for me that in order to develop the capacity in myself that I so longed for, I needed to dig deep and do my own personal work.

Wanting Isn't Enough

Wanting something isn't enough. Saying we are something isn't enough. We absolutely have to develop it. And, it turns out, we have to keep developing ourselves throughout our lives because our challenges change and we continually want to maintain and expand our full range of being.

This book is a resource that I would have liked when I was in my teens and twenties. Though I found some role models of women who displayed personal power, there was no *roadmap* for how to develop it in myself. Emulating what I saw in them only got me so far.

And I know from my work with women of all ages, we do not automatically develop personal power as we age and mature. I know women in their thirties, forties, and fifties who are still struggling to trust themselves, to use personal power at work and in their relationships, to be authentic and transparent without evaluating themselves as weak.

This book is that roadmap.

As a lifelong student of human psychology and a body-oriented therapist for more than two decades, I've amassed multiple holistic strategies that will enable you to grow your power and have a greater impact in the world. Reflective journaling, body position practices, decision-making analysis, and body awareness inventories are among the strategies I guide you through to support you on your journey to achieving power.

You may want to invest in a journal, or, I provide all the above-mentioned strategies in a single, complimentary workbook that you can download for by visiting www.NancyJonker.com/Resources. The workbook provides a succinct space for you to easily locate the strategies I recommend and for you to create a compilation of your journey that you can return to for years to come.

As you go through these strategies and record your reflections, your workbook or journal will transform into your personal roadmap to a more powerful and satisfying life.

Young women in their teens, twenties, and thirties, as well as women in their forties, fifties and sixties have used these time-tested strategies to think on their feet, improve their relationships by speaking up and holding their own, and increase their credibility and impact in the workplace.

Kathryn's Story—
From "Wanna Be" to Be

Kathryn, a twenty-six-year-old radiology technician, approached me because she wanted to empower herself both at work and at home. She knew what she wanted but needed guidance on how to achieve it.

After working with me using the same practices I share in this book, Kathryn now reports, "I no longer have panic attacks or anxiety I can't control. I'm functioning better at work, I'm less overwhelmed and more organized. These tools help me in my relationship with my husband and my mom, staying clear about what are my issues and what are theirs."

With targeted assistance, Kathryn was able to move from a "wanna be" phase to a place of actual achievement. It's sometimes tempting to stay in the "wanna be" phase—"I wanna be an independent woman, so I'm going to pretend that I am and put up a good facade." Or "I wanna get off this treadmill of protecting perceptions, but I don't think I can."

In so many areas of life (organization, fitness, health), it's easier to think about BEING something than BECOMING something. Perhaps you know of those who dream of being fit, but don't want to start going to the gym and face their actual level of fitness. Or you may know those who want to live a simplified lifestyle, but don't relish the idea of actually simplifying.

Don't get caught in the "wanna be" phase.

Become that woman that teen girls look up to and want to emulate. Become that woman that other powerful women want to get to know and hang around with. Become that woman who gives younger women a hand because you developed your capacity to hold your own, to speak your mind, and to have an impact. Become that leader the world needs. And become that woman who could attract any partner!

The Roadmap Defined

In this book, we will talk about the seven dimensions of personal power and what the anchors look like at each end of the continuum. We'll look at the stories of women who show varying degrees of personal power to flesh out important concepts.

We'll take a look at what the barriers are to having and developing personal power and some of our attitudes that need to shift. Then we'll cover three skills that are critical for developing personal power. We'll review potent methods for building these essential skills.

Finally, we'll talk about my POWER formula and review holistic strategies for not only developing personal power, but consistently using it across the different arenas of life. Of course, we'll talk about the benefits of doing so—how it helps us take more risks, live more fully, have more fun, and be more effective.

If you read the guide below and practice the strategies provided, you'll see an improvement in your ability to function effectively in this world. You'll be able to stand on your own two feet, recover when "the rug gets pulled out from under you," and keep a clear head even when you feel guilty or are challenged about a decision you've made.

You'll also be able to step out of the box of the self-reliant woman who can't afford to be vulnerable or show who you really are. You'll learn ways to stay connected to your very best strengths while allowing yourself to be approachable and human.

Don't wait for someone to give you permission to be fully yourself—develop and exude all of your strength and all of your feminine softness.

Onward we go!

Chapter 2:
What Is Personal Power?
Identifying the 7 Dimensions

> *One of the most courageous things you can do is identify yourself, know who you are, what you believe in and where you want to go.*
> —Sheila Murray Bethel

Perhaps the easiest way to address the seven dimensions of personal power is to look at them depicted in the life of Sarah.

Sarah's Story

Meet Sarah, a 35-year-old photographer, mother of two, wife, daughter, friend, and volunteer. Sarah loves photography, in general, and, in particular, likes to capture intimate moments between mother and child, husband and wife, or lovers in general.

Sarah has a part-time photography business that she runs out of her home where she also cares for her two young children. Sarah's husband, Tom, is supportive of her but doesn't always know what to do to help.

Despite the many good things in Sarah's life, her happiness quotient is not high. She is plagued by indecision, missed deadlines, and anxiety around scheduling her photo shoots. To make up for some of these shortcomings, she charges her clients less than other professionals of her caliber and discusses financial matters as little as possible.

Though Sarah's friends and family tell her she is extraordinarily talented and should charge more for her work, Sarah is not at all confident of this. She takes classes and attends workshops to improve her skill. Every now and then, she feels resentment when she sees other photographers' work displayed but consoles herself with the reminder that she works part-time.

Sarah's children, in kindergarten and preschool, demand much of her time and attention. She worries and often feels guilty about not being with them when they're not in school. Yet, even when she's with them, she's often scattered, exhausted, and overwhelmed with tasks unfinished. She longs for a system that would help her stay organized and focused.

Sarah's relationship with her husband, Tom, is steady overall, but filled with nitpicky kinds of conflicts. They seem to keep an unwritten tally of who is doing what and contributing the most.

Sarah often feels lonely, is resentful of Tom's long work hours, and frequently asks that she and the kids be made more of a priority. In the evenings, when Sarah is alone, she often gets a case of the jitters and eats to calm herself and to ease the loneliness she feels.

Holidays and extended family gatherings are a struggle, as Sarah and Tom must decide when to visit each of their families. Sarah is uncertain how to make these decisions and often defers to Tom's preferences or her mother's wishes. She vacillates between the two, lacking a strategy to figure out what she really wants. Sarah dreads the onset of the holiday season.

Sarah values fitness and tries to find time to exercise and eat well. Before she had children, she worked out three to four times a week and ate a plant-rich diet. More recently, however, Sarah eats mac n' cheese with her kids and struggles to work out even two times a week. She doesn't know where her energy goes. Sex is something she rarely thinks about, and she and Tom make love only when he initiates.

Sarah often worries about being taken advantage of and is quick to stand up for herself with friends. When conflicts arise, she takes a broad stroke approach, letting her friends know that she was wronged. She seems uncertain about how to resolve such conflicts, as she does not want to be seen as giving in. Friendships seem a bit tricky to her and she often wishes to feel more connected to people than she does.

Lessons about Personal Power

Sarah's story, while not typical in all its dimensions, helps us see where she lacks personal power. Her story also portrays how having good things in life, like a steady relationship with a spouse, healthy children, talents in a particular field, and a good income, don't necessarily add up to living a life with confidence and power.

Sarah's story also illustrates how many of these dimensions are intertwined. For purposes of clarity, we will separate them into 7 distinct, yet interrelated, dimensions and talk about each of them in turn.

At the end of this section, there are instructions how to set up these continuums in your journal. Alternatively, the free companion workbook has these continuums set up and labeled for you.

Go to www.NancyJonker.com/Workbook to download the free workbook.

The 7 Dimensions of Personal Power

- Cognitive Functioning
- Emotional Functioning
- Boundaries
- Personal Energy
- Relationship Quality
- Finances
- Capacity for Taking Risks

1. Cognitive Functioning

The first dimension, *cognitive functioning*, includes things like being decisive, clear-headed, and able to call upon your mental faculties. It also includes being relatively free of distortions in our reasoning. That is to say, not being prone to overgeneralizations or "catastrophizing," and being able to accurately discriminate between what is real and what is not.

The other end of this continuum is indecisiveness, difficulty concentrating, being mentally scattered, and having a tendency to ruminate. Rumination is the excessive worry that can plague us well before or after an interaction.

Rumination can be a symptom of shame as we continually replay the interaction in our minds while almost jumping out of our skin, wishing we had said this, wondering if saying that was okay.

Shame tells us we not only did something wrong, stupid, or embarrassing—it goes a step further, declaring that we are a worthless, idiotic person. Shame is an example of a cognitive distortion and how it may be difficult to discriminate between what is real and what is our distorted sense of what's real.

With Sarah, we see that her *cognitive functioning* is characterized by indecision and rumination. She is continually evaluating herself and her interactions with others, sometimes falling into shame, sometimes just worrying. She is unclear about her value overall and the value of the work she does.

2. Emotional Functioning

Sometimes we actually choose worry over other painful or difficult feelings. This transitions us into the realm of *emotional functioning*. So this aspect of *emotional functioning* is about being able to move on from mistakes, to stay clear about who we are and our sense of worth, and to navigate the highs and the lows of life without tipping over.

Having personal power in the emotional realm means having the ability to regulate our feelings and their expression without getting overwhelmed by them. Having an inner fortitude that enables us to withstand the ups and downs and to have enough capacity within ourselves to feel happiness, sadness, pain, grief, loneliness and anger, all without becoming undone.

So on the one side of the *emotional functioning* continuum we would write:

- Inner fortitude
- Emotional regulation
- Ability to experience range of emotions without being overwhelmed

On the opposite side of the continuum we would write:

- Inability to experience range of emotions
- Difficulty regulating or transitioning out of intense feelings
- Overwhelmed
- Unstable fluctuations in mood and feelings

Sarah's *emotional functioning* is characterized by self-doubt, anxiety, guilt, and feeling overwhelmed. In the evenings she has trouble settling down and often engages in "comfort eating" to alleviate her loneliness.

She feels resentful of other photographers' success and of her husband's long work hours, and seems unaware of how these resentments could inform and guide her decisions about her own desires and goals.

We will talk in later chapters about how to develop the capacity for self-regulation and how to have and express feelings without getting consumed by them. So stay tuned because this is an all-important area of personal power.

3. Boundaries

Boundaries, the third dimension of personal power, are the container for all the energy that flows within us. Just as our skin keeps our muscles, blood vessels, and tissues intact, our personal *boundaries* help us own and channel our energy.

Boundaries can be as simple as the capacity to say yes or no—to someone begging on the street or to a request that we head up a new project. *Boundaries* serve our personal power by keeping a rein on our energy, so that we choose where and with whom to spend our precious time and limited resources.

On the one side of the *boundaries* continuum, we would write:

- Capacity for differentiation (more on this coming up)
- Capacity to protect physical boundaries

- Capacity to protect time and energy

On the opposite side of the *boundaries* continuum, we would write:

- Tendency to lose oneself, one's needs, and/or one's preferences
- Limited ability to protect physical boundaries
- Limited ability to protect time and energy

In Sarah's story, we see that *boundaries* are challenging for her. She struggles a bit with differentiation—being able to soothe herself when alone, being able to talk productively to resolve relationship conflicts, and being able to decide her own preferences around holidays and other gatherings. She may tend toward a rigid, one-size-fits-all style of boundaries (more on that later) that leaves her feeling more disconnected than she likes.

4. Personal Energy

Personal energy, the fourth dimension of personal power, is really about how able we are to focus where our energy goes and how it flows. Are we in charge? Or is our energy spent suppressing feelings from the past, cutting us off from present-day opportunities?

Do we have the ability to channel our energy where we want (such as taking a class, taking on a new project, or having coffee with a friend). Can we direct how it flows in our bodies? Or do we get cut off from our bodies and chase thoughts endlessly round and round in our heads?

On our continuum of personal energy, on one side we would write:

- Energy available for current opportunities
- Energy able to flow freely in the body

Energy that is able to flow freely in the body is characterized by pulsation—dynamic movement in the vertical dimension (up through the ground, all the way up and through us with a forward and outward movement) and in the horizontal dimension—a pulsating, expansive breath. A good flow of energy is characterized by aliveness in the body, easy natural breathing, and good sexual functioning.

On the opposite side of the personal energy continuum, we would write:

- Energy drained by suppressing feelings and/or conflicts from the past
- Energy locked up and unable to flow

When energy is drained or locked up, there is a lack of aliveness in the body and sometimes an accumulation of tension in the muscles—often the neck and shoulders.

Sarah's *personal energy* is characterized by feeling drained and exhausted. She no longer works out as she used to and has trouble making decisions that foster her own health and well-being.

This is partly a boundary issue that impacts her available energy. She may also be low on energy because she's avoiding conflicts with her husband and within herself. Unattended conflicts create quite the drain on our energy.

5. Relationship Quality

The *quality of our relationship*s is another indicator of our empowerment quotient. When empowered, we are able to hold our own, connect with our partner or loved ones, gather with friends, and all the while NOT LOSE SIGHT of OURSELVES. This process is called differentiation.

For many of us, it may not be all that hard to be with someone, and it may not be all that hard to be with ourselves. But to stay in touch with ourselves AND connect with someone at the same time is the real challenge.

Especially when we're with people we love and connect deeply with, we can become more attuned to them and their needs than to ourselves and our needs. "Differentiation," as described by David Schnarch in his book, *Passionate Marriage,* "involves balancing two basic life forces: the drive for individuality and the drive for togetherness" (55).

This essential, yet difficult, skill is one we can work on over our entire lives. Indeed, as our relationship becomes more important to us, our need for differentiation—the ability to stand on our own two feet as an individual—increases.

So on the continuum of *relationship quality,* on one side we would write:

- Capacity and desire for connection and mutuality
- Capacity for differentiation (again)
- Capacity for raising conflicts and expecting resolution

On the opposite side of the continuum, we would write:

- Lack of mutuality (an it's-me-or-you approach to conflicts)
- Relationships characterized by distance or by clinginess (lack of differentiation) or a

fluctuation between the two (come close, go away)
- Disinclination to voice disagreement, no expectation for resolution

For Sarah, her personal power on the *relationship quality* dimension is mixed. She tends to avoid conflicts with her husband, often deferring to his preferences because she doesn't want to create conflict or does not expect resolution.

Sarah lives with multiple small irritants that are likely the result of those larger, unaddressed conflicts. Her sense of self is tenuous enough that it is difficult for her to be truly differentiated—that is, both emotionally close and emotionally capable of being on her own.

6. Finances

Personal power in the *financial* realm is about being *financially* informed—knowing where your money goes, being able to live within your means, not drowning in debt or living paycheck to paycheck, and being paid what you're worth. It's also about knowing you can go out and earn the money you need. That sounds like empowerment, doesn't it?

On the one end of the *finances* continuum, we would write:

- Financially informed
- Able to live within means
- Realistic or productive debt
- Income commensurate with value (paid what you're worth)
- Able to have conversations around finances

On the opposing end of the continuum, we would write:

- Uninformed, inattentive to finances, tendency to defer financial matters to others
- Living beyond means
- Unproductive or large amounts of debt
- Not paid according to worth
- Inability or unwillingness to have conversations around finances (with partner, children, or boss)

Financial empowerment is an area often overlooked by women, especially within the home. There is a strong tendency for women to defer to their partners in the *financial* arena, often because they feel less capable.

Or women may track their *financials* at work, but take a more hands-off approach at home. This is a critical area of personal power, and I encourage all women to know their *financial* situations and be involved! Find a financial planner you're comfortable with, or read books, so you can be educated and informed.

Sarah's personal power on the financial dimension is relatively low. Her self-doubt about her worth translates into charging less than other photographers of her caliber. She also compensates financially for her missed deadlines and difficulties scheduling.

Sarah doesn't talk openly about money with either her clients or her partner. We might expect that if Sarah demonstrated more personal power in some of these other areas, she might feel better about charging what she is worth and having those necessary conversations.

7. Capacity for Taking Risks

Capacity for risk-taking, the seventh dimension of personal power, includes a willingness to be vulnerable, to move forward with your goals and desires, to be authentically "out there" and not hide. Sometimes we don't know our inner desires, but, when we do, the question becomes whether we're willing to pursue them.

On the continuum of *capacity for taking risks*, we would write on one side:

- Willingness to be vulnerable

- Willingness to be authentic
- Willingness to risk failure (and trust our resilience)

On the other side, we would write:

- Tendency to hide
- Tendency to play it safe, avoid risking rejection or failure.

Sarah's *capacity for taking risks* seems fairly low. She is attentive to her skill development as a photographer, but doesn't really go for it. She treats her work more like a hobby and doesn't reap the rewards that she'd like.

Journal Junction: The 7 Dimensions and You

In response to these the seven aspects of personal power, let's pause, reflect, and write.

As with every strategy, exercise, and Journal Junction given in this book, this writing exercise is available and already formatted for you, in the free companion workbook. The workbook lays out these seven continuums, along with their detailed characteristics, so you can easily begin the task of rating yourself in each of the seven aspects of power. Go to www.NancyJonker.com/Workbook to download the workbook.

The other option is to create these continuums yourself. To do this, you'll take out a journal, draw seven lines, and put a 1 at the left side of each line and a ten at the right side. Then you will label each line with one of the seven dimensions of personal power.

Now go ahead and rate yourself on each of these dimensions. Use the detailed characteristics given for each dimension to help you better evaluate yourself. You might be tempted to be way too hard on yourself, so watch that.

For some, you might have really different answers depending on whether you're talking about your work or personal life. Feel free to rate these separately, one for home and another for work, and then give yourself an overall rating in that category.

Your journaling here might take 10–30 minutes. If you find it hard to do, you can go one of two ways. You can do the quick overview approach and just go with your inclination without thinking too hard or too much about it.

Alternatively, you can really delve into the exercise, using it to explore these aspects of your life with some depth. You may decide to write about certain aspects that may have pleasantly surprised or troubled you. In addition, you may want to talk your discoveries over with a trusted friend or someone who is also interested in developing more personal power.

The important take-away of this exercise is to develop awareness of these various capacities within you. In the process of building greater personal power, you want some kind of a benchmark of where you are right now. And at the end of this journey, you'll see how your capabilities can and will increase across these different dimensions.

Up Next . . .

In the next section, we're going to talk about five widely held beliefs among women that limit personal power and may even stop the desire for developing more personal power. We'll talk about two more beliefs that can have quite a destructive impact, especially when they exist below the level of conscious awareness. So do the rating exercise, then read on!

Chapter 3:
Five Limiting Beliefs, Plus Two Destructive Beliefs

The most common way people give up their power is by thinking they don't have any.
—Alice Walker

So why don't all women possess personal power? Why are some more empowered than others? Why are some women more advanced in all seven dimensions of power while some struggle with all but one?

Why are some women able to say what needs to be said in the moment while others go home and ponder, wishing they had said what finally comes to them?

What does it take to be able to think on your feet? To trust your judgment in the face of opposition and challenge? To go with your intuition even when it breaks the norm? What allows us to be able to speak up and ask for what we want or what we think is fair?

In my readings and in my work with women over the years, I've identified five beliefs that seriously limit the development of personal power. I'm confident you'll recognize them as soon as I name them.

Until we challenge these beliefs and resolve them, we will limit how powerful we can be in the world, and we will continue to limit the amount of impact we have.

Five Beliefs that Limit Personal Power

- Selfishness is bad and hurts those you love.
- Ambition makes you bitchy.
- Guilt should be avoided at all cost.
- Strength means not showing weakness.
- Self-compassion is self-indulgent.

So who doesn't want to have personal power? Surprisingly, many of us shy away from the prospect of being powerful. When I talk with my clients about this, many of them don't think of themselves as powerful and aren't even comfortable with the term. Many of us have attitudes about selfishness, ambition, strength, self-compassion, and self-love that not only interfere with our acting in powerful ways, but also curb our desire to become powerful.

Most of us, if we drilled down even deeper, would find that we have core assumptions about ourselves that sound something like these: "I'm not enough" or "I'm not worthy"—therefore I must give, therefore I must defer, therefore I must bend over backwards to make things happen for my family, for my friends, for my co-workers or boss.

The Narrow Bandwidth of Acceptability

When I was exploring the whole phenomenon of shame, I found that for myself and many women I talked with, shame lurks on either side of an attitude or aspiration. What I mean by this is we allow ourselves a moderate amount of a quality but monitor ourselves so as not to have too much or go overboard. One example of this is ambition.

No one dreams of being completely lacking in ambition. Without it we might sit around on the couch all day and not have goals we strive to reach. We would likely feel shame if we had no ambition at all. But, if we exhibit a high degree of ambition, we might also feel shame. When someone tells you that you're "very ambitious," it can be hard to know whether this is a compliment or an insult.

This is true for a number of other qualities as well. Think about the ability to make money. If you bring in no money (even if this is your pre-planned arrangement in your relationship), it can take a toll on self-esteem. Many women struggle with this and may begin to defer to their partner (even subconsciously) because they feel less than equal in their relationship.

But on the flip side, women aren't necessarily comfortable making a lot of money either. Even if you enjoy good things that flow from having an abundant income, you might also feel slightly embarrassed or ashamed about making so much.

When women are looking ahead and setting their income goals, they tend to put a ceiling on their goals. This is often the result of hidden shame. Hidden because women have no idea it's there, but it's influencing their decisions nonetheless. It takes attentiveness to the financial arena to develop or remain at a high level of functioning on this dimension of personal power.

It's important to explore what your attitudes are about being healthy, physically fit, physically attractive, ambitious, selfish, and self-compassionate. Look at these in some detail, exploring what your attitudes are about having an abundance of these qualities versus little to none. And see if you, too, restrict what you allow yourself.

Here are some examples of how we might keep ourselves within a narrow range. With regard to fitness, "I can be focused on my fitness to some extent, but if I really made it a priority, I would seem obsessed or self-centered."

In terms of ambition, "It's okay for me to have goals, but if I start really focusing on achievement, I might get 'too big for my britches.'" (Is anyone else familiar with that term and with that concern?)

Regarding financial success, "I want to be paid fairly for my work, but I'm not comfortable being paid more than I'm worth." Women in particular have concerns about their value and often underestimate their worth.

With regard to clarity, "It's okay to say what I want as long as I don't sound mean." So many women I know curb their clarity and assertiveness out of a fear of being or sounding mean. What is the real fear behind this? In what ways are our lives worse off if someone experiences us as mean? Perhaps this is, at its deepest level, a fear of being rejected and alone.

Let's consider each belief in turn and how it limits our desire and development of personal power. Grab your journal, so you can explore your own attitudes and beliefs and see where they might limit you.

Belief #1: Selfishness Is Bad and Hurts Those We Love.

Consider Jill who longs to start a business but feels she can't use family funds to get the training she needs. If we talked with Jill, we might find out she believes anything smacking of selfishness is bad. She might tell us that her mother often instructed her not to be selfish, to look out for her sister's feelings, and to accommodate her goals accordingly.

At the time of writing this, I was prepared to put in a good word for selfishness. To question how it got such a bad rap! But then I looked it up in the dictionary and saw that the definition is completely negative! "Self-interest" was portrayed equally poorly. Yet, of course, we have to attend to our own self-interest. If we do not, who will?

We need to distinguish between productive selfishness—acting with prudent self-interest versus blatant, uncaring selfishness. Productive selfishness is when you act in your own best interest as a way of taking care of yourself.

Productive selfishness can actually make you more generous! It's a common misunderstanding, especially among women, that selfishness in any degree makes us self-centered and hurts those we love.

In actuality, however, when we make decisions that serve our best interest, we can free up our time and energy for those we love. We come to our loved ones in a less depleted state. We show up because we want to be there and while we still have something left in our tank.

Acting through productive selfishness actually helps us gain personal power in practically all of the seven dimensions, and, in particular, increases our personal energy, capacity for taking risks, and ability to set clear boundaries. And that makes all the difference. Being selfish can actually help those we love.

Journal Junction:
On Selfishness

In the complimentary workbook or your journal, take 5–10 minutes to write about the role of "selfishness" in your life. What is your attitude about productive selfishness? What *opportunities* that promoted your positive self-interest have you accepted or denied? What was the aftermath of accepting/rejecting the opportunities? Take some time to figure out your stance around this common belief.

Belief #2: Ambition Makes Us Bitchy.

While we're examining attitudes, we've got to look at ambition. Just notice what you feel inside when you read the word. Any little jolt in your gut? Anything get fired up?

When you think about leading with your ambition, what's your reaction and what reaction do you anticipate from others? Maybe you anticipate judgment about having a big ego, maybe a little suspicion.

In my own life, a little ambition, if it wasn't too noticeable, was acceptable, but having a lot of it raised suspicion among my family and friends, sometimes creating envy, sometimes distance, and sometimes outright criticism.

Yet we know in our heart of hearts that ambition is good. Ambition creates drive and is fueled by desire. Our ambition can lead us to tackle fears, to stretch into territory we might never otherwise venture.

This certainly increases our personal power in our capacity for risk-taking as well as increasing our personal power in cognitive and emotional functioning. If you have negative attitudes about ambition, it's time to explore them deeply, so you can let them go. It's time to embrace your ambition without apology or reserve.

Journal Junction: On Ambition

In your workbook or journal, take 5–10 minutes to write about "ambition" in your life. Write about a time when you or a woman you know acted on your/her ambition. What was the response? What are you ambitious to do? What ambitions have you buried and what ambitions have you pursued? Explore the relationship between your ambition and how it relates to your levels of power in each of the seven dimensions.

Belief #3: Guilt Should Be Avoided at All Costs.

Consider Rachael, who continues to say yes to volunteering at her kids' school, even though she wants to do less and be with her kids more. Rachael might tell us that if she said no, even if the reason for saying no was to spend more time with her family, she would feel guilty, which for her is just as bad as feeling overworked.

Countless women that I have worked with over the years have told me that they cannot make different decisions regarding their life, often with regard to their families, because they would feel too guilty. The guilt would ruin whatever experience they were trying to create for themselves, so it would not be worth it.

Here it's important to distinguish between the short view and the long haul. When asked, probably none of us would say we should allow guilt to dictate our behavior. We might even scoff at the idea of guilt running the show. (Or we might nod our heads in commiseration!)

In a later chapter, we're going to talk about the repetition compulsion and how it compels us to continue with the status quo—even while presenting us with repeated opportunities to make things different.

Guilt is one of the feelings that keeps us locked in the status quo. Guilt keeps our power in the dimensions of boundaries, personal energy, capacity for taking risks, and emotional functioning quite low.

The remedy for this? We must learn to tolerate the discomfort of guilt in favor of acting in accordance with our inner wisdom and desire. Is this an easy thing to do, especially in the beginning? Not at all! But, if you can learn to tolerate guilt in the short run, you create freedom and choice for yourself down the road.

So for Rachael, even if she feels guilty about choosing to do less at her kids' school and it interferes with her enjoyment of her time at home, it *breaks the cycle* of making decisions based on guilt. The next time she chooses something by carefully checking her inner voice, she will have a little easier time with the guilty feelings that follow. And the next time, maybe a little less. This is how change happens. And this is how we break the bonds of guilt and increase our personal power in a multitude of dimensions!

We will talk more about this in Chapter 5 where I'll introduce a useful tool for determining what really is motivating our behavior. But for now, think about incrementally shifting out of letting guilt decide!

Journal Junction:
On Guilt

Explore the place of "guilt" in your life. In your workbook or journal, take 5–10 minutes to write about a time when guilt motivated you to do (or not do) something. Explore how guilt plays a role in both big and small ways in your life, how it affects you in terms of your boundaries, personal energy, capacity for taking risks, and emotional functioning. Where and when can you say no to guilt and yes to yourself more often? What would the consequences be? Write about it.

Belief #4: Strength Means Not Showing Weakness (and Not Being Vulnerable).

Sitting with Caroline, I heard a familiar story. She was talking about her exhaustion at work and at professional conferences. She was fighting with herself and her own anxiety, willing it not to show when she spoke in front of others. In exploring this, she expressed her fear that if her weakness showed, she would not be selected as a leader in her field and would ultimately be rejected.

How many of us don't worry about this? How many of us worry if there are any chinks in our armor, we will get passed over, denied, rejected, or fired? It is such a common story that I hear. Many of us really believe that strength is a complete absence of weakness and that any show of vulnerability is unacceptable.

Yet, when I asked Caroline what she would look for in choosing a person to mentor and bring into leadership roles, she was clear that she would not be as put off by someone else's weakness as she is by her own. In fact, she would see this as an opportunity to help a younger professional and an opportunity to make a real impact.

We tend to be hard on ourselves with regard to our weaknesses. To us, they are like neon signs telling the world about our insecurities and flaws. Yet maybe the biggest weakness of all is not having the courage to face ourselves and the fact that we are not perfect and never can be. The quest for perfection is really about trying to avoid pain.

Strength without weakness hardly allows us to be our authentic selves. We cannot be transparent while we are hiding. We cannot fully own our power when we're afraid of what people might see.

We will talk more about this in Chapter 8, but owning and emphasizing our strengths does not mean disowning our weaknesses or vulnerabilities. It means making peace with our imperfections, doing what we can to grow while coming face to face with our fears of being rejected.

When we can face these fears, we can stop trying to protect our image, and we can run with our strengths, which in turn will increase the quality of our relationships, our emotional functioning, our personal energy, and our capacity for taking risks. We'll talk about how exactly to discover and expand into our strengths when we review the POWER formula.

Journal Junction: Strength and Vulnerability

Explore your attitude about strength and vulnerability. In your workbook or journal, take 5–10 minutes to describe a situation in which you did or did not show your vulnerability and the results of that. Write about the role of weakness in your quest to be strong. In what relationships and situations do you have the best and worst balance?

Belief #5: Self-Compassion Is Self-Indulgent.

In my clinical practice, I often raise the idea of self-compassion. There has been a surge of research on this topic by Kristin Neff and others, and it proves to be profoundly helpful.

Yet you should see the looks and the eye rolls when I first bring it up! Back to this idea about being strong and vulnerable—compassion aimed at the self has a connotation of being hopelessly soft and self-indulgent. We fear that compassion toward ourselves will make us into couch potatoes. We fear that without the criticism we pour on, we'll be aimless, lazy, and ineffective.

Journal Junction:
On Self-Compassion

For now, just notice and take a few minutes to write about your attitudes toward self-compassion. Use one of these sentence starters:

- If I were more compassionate with myself, I might . . .
- If I treated myself more like I treat a friend, I might . . .

Add ten or so endings to the one you choose and see what your subconscious has to tell you. Try to expand your thinking, so you see not only how compassion toward yourself might seem counterproductive for you but also how it might help you. You'll find this Journal Junction conveniently laid out in the workbook for your exploration of the positive side of self-compassion.

We will be talking in greater detail about self-compassion in later chapters, exploring how it differs from self-esteem and what's involved in the practice of extending compassion toward ourselves. We'll take a look at what the research has to say about self-compassion too—because it's clearly not self-indulgent!

Plus Two Destructive Beliefs

In addition to these five widely held beliefs that can seriously hamper our development of personal power are two other beliefs shared among some of us. These may not be as widely held as the others, but they need to be included because the repercussions from them are so destructive. These beliefs are "I Can't Trust What I Know" and "I'm the Problem."

Belief #6: I Can't Trust What I Know.

How do we know what we know? And how do we come to trust it? How many of us were actually taught to seek out and value our ideas, feelings, and beliefs? How many of us were told, when we said we were cold, hot, or hurting, that we could not be—because it was not cold, hot, or there was no reason for hurting? Without ever being told directly to mistrust ourselves, we got the message to mistrust ourselves, what our bodies were telling us, and what our inner voice was telling us.

Mistrusting ourselves leads to devaluing ourselves. It also impacts our sense of reality. Afterall, if you're told time and time again that what you feel is not the way it is or that your mother or brother or someone else older and wiser than you has a hold on reality and you do not, it makes you question whether what you perceive is real. This, in turn, greatly decreases your personal power in so many dimensions—your cognitive functioning, your emotional functioning, your sense of boundaries, your personal energy, and your capacity for taking risks.

Developing a trust in your own sense of reality is especially difficult when there are family secrets that the family system is protecting. These can vary in degree from minor, such as an incident from the past that's embarrassing to talk about so no one does, to major, such as alcoholism or abuse, past or present. When the family is keeping secrets, the result on the person growing up in that environment is often a developmental deficit of being able to know, test, or trust reality.

Being unable to trust our own sense of reality makes us vulnerable. Vulnerable to relationships with men who use power to their own advantage. These men may tell us things and even if what they say doesn't ring true, we might accept it anyway. When what we're told doesn't conform to how we feel, we tend to go inward and question, question, question—"Am I being the stubborn one here?", "Maybe I am being cold-hearted," "Am I expecting too much?"—and on the questions go.

A malleable sense of reality is one of the most significant challenges to being empowered because we tend to question everything within us. This untenable sense of reality walks hand in hand with devaluing the self and the information available to us. We become dependent on validation from those outside ourselves.

In the best-case scenarios, this means we rely on the love and good intentions of our partners to take into consideration what we want along with what they want. In the worst-case scenarios, this mistrust of reality can leave us susceptible to abuses of power.

The subtlety of this problem is what makes it so dangerous. When women don't know they suffer from mistrusting their sense of reality, they accept the reality told to them—over and over and over again. They continue to believe that they are the problem (after all, if it's not cold in here and you're cold, you must be off somehow). And this leads to the related and equally destructive belief, "I'm the Problem."

Belief #7: I'm the Problem.

As long as women believe they're the problem, they cannot effectively confront or challenge the reality presented by another. Worst-case scenarios with a malleable sense of reality include domestic violence. But more subtle forms include misuse of power within a relationship where the confidence of the woman is eroded.

In my practice and in my life, I see the damage this deficit and the resulting attitude of "I must be the problem" does. It is pernicious and requires that a woman who suffers from a malleable sense of reality must surround herself with clear-headed people who can see the situation she's in, who know who she truly is, and regularly provide her an accurate "read" on reality.

A commonplace example of this is the malfunctioning gas gauge in my sons' Honda Civic. The gas gauge has been broken since we got the car, so the boys have learned not to depend on it. They track their gas consumption, miles driven, and time of last fill-up as the reliable indicators of gas in the tank.

So it is when our sense of reality malfunctions because it has been messed with. The first step in dealing with it is to be aware that there's a problem. You get the bind here though, right? It feels like an awful state to be in.

Once you know you don't trust your own perceptions of reality, whether they're trustworthy or not, you don't just flip a switch and start trusting it. This is something you have to develop (unlike the gas gauge that will never be accurate unless replaced). And since we're talking about such a pervasive, important ability, we discover we're quite vulnerable in this window of time between becoming aware of the problem and having a solution.

Women who are in partnerships where they are constantly being told they are the problem have a particularly poignant challenge. They tend to lose confidence in their own perceptions and feel beaten down. They are unsure whether their take on the situation is worthy of their trust. This is how such a difficult cycle ensues.

When this happens, it is imperative to find other reliable indicators of reality while doing everything possible to rebuild trust in your inner voice, your sensations, and internal messages. During this critical time, it is important to identify a person (or two) in your life who sees you *most* clearly and has an accurate read on your situation. If you rely on too many people, you will end up in confusion again.

So pick one or two clear-headed people you trust who have a strong investment in you. Maybe this is a good friend, a sister or brother, a mentor, or a therapist. Establish an understanding that you will need to do brief reality checks on a frequent basis to keep your perceptions clear. Get their agreement to participate for a set period of time to help you grow this capacity.

Not only is it crucial to rebuild trust in ourselves, we need to make our inner knowing as accurate as possible. This requires easy and ready access to what we know inside, so we need to build a bridge between our heads and our hearts and keep the access clear.

Journal Junction:
Plus 2 More

Take a few minutes to write about these last two beliefs—*I can't trust what I know* and *I'm the problem*—in the complimentary workbook or your journal. Explore how any aspect of these two beliefs may be present in your life, whether in a big or very small way. Describe how these beliefs impact your choices, decisions, and actions.

Up Next . . .

In the next chapter we'll explore how to build a bridge between our head, heart, and gut. Our way of getting acquainted with our inner selves is often through the body. We'll go through some body awareness exercises to open our minds and senses to the myriad of information available to us about what we know and feel

Chapter 4:
Building the Bridge between Head and Heart

> *It is only by grounding our awareness in the living sensation of our bodies that the "I Am," our real presence, can awaken.*
> —G. I. Gurdjieff

We know we need easy, clear access to what our inner voice is telling us and need to develop trust in what our inner wisdom is telling us. How do we do this? Fortunately, we have what we need with us all the time—we just have to learn and be willing to tune in.

Self-Awareness Follows Body-Awareness

Boundaries and Bodily Cues— An Exercise

Try this exercise:

First, you'll need the help of someone you know and like.

Stand on one side of the room. Have this person slowly walk toward you—slowly enough that you can tell them when to stop. When they get "close enough" tell them to stop.

Now reflect on HOW you knew they were "close enough."

What in your body told you?

Did your breath get shallow? Did your eyes go wonky, feeling like they wanted to move back into your head?) Did you feel a tension in your chest? A tightening in your gut? A subtle backing away with your head?

Now play with it. Have the person move back a step or two. Have them move forward and back if you like. Notice what happens in your body. What changes? Where do you feel it?

Then have them come close again.

This is body awareness. Our bodies are giving us clues and information all day long.

We need to attune our ears. We need to focus our inner vision. We need to pay attention and be willing to accept what we learn. In so doing, we can increase our personal power in our cognitive and emotional functioning, as well as our boundaries and personal energy.

Journal Junction:
Your Bodily Cues

This is a great time to jot a few notes in your workbook or journal about what you tuned into. Maybe you're already good at this and have had lots of practice. Or maybe you've been living in your head because you find it too painful to tune into your body. Write down what you noticed about yourself from this exercise.

Maybe you're ready to start, however slowly, claiming the information and wisdom your body can share with you. Make a note about your attitudes toward your body and the information available.

Taking Inventory: A Slow Journey
Through the Body

This next exercise is all about focusing inward, so I have created an mp3 available for you to download. This way, you can tune into yourself with your eyes closed if you'd like to focus on the exercise without having to read it. Go to www.NancyJonker.com/MP3 to download the mp3.

Once we tune into our bodies, we can have quite the treasure hunt! Let's try going top to bottom and see what's available to us. Let's start with our eyes. We might notice them tightening, hardening, growing wide (usually in fear or surprise), or feeling a pressure behind them, possibly a buildup of unshed tears.

Next, the lips and the jaw. Think back to that exercise—or do it again. Do your lips change at all when someone draws near? Maybe they become tight and thin (tight-lipped, when we suppress what we want to say). Maybe they're pursed in consternation. And the jaw—we can clamp it down purposefully or tighten it unconsciously.

The neck and throat can also provide us information. Maybe the muscles around our throat get tight and constricted. See if you can gauge your voice on the continuum of full-throated to pinched, breathy, raspy, or tight.

One of the easiest ways to hear your clear vocal sound is to pretend that there's someone in the street who is going to get hit unless you get their attention. So without thinking much about it, yell, "HEY!" This instantly engages the diaphragm and opens your throat. You can then compare this sound to the more familiar sound you make to see how open or constricted your throat typically is.

The muscles supporting the head also have something to tell us. Maybe they bend to one side (and always to the same side, of course!). Maybe they're always a little contracted in the back, making our chin point up just a little. Notice whatever you can now and in the days ahead about just how your head is supported by your neck.

Moving to the chest, a place of breathing and also the heart center. To start, just notice how the chest feels. Heavy? Like there's a weight sitting on it? Light? Do you feel open? Protected? Many of us have a desire to protect ourselves and our tender, vulnerable heart feelings.

Along with this, notice what your arms are inclined to do. Do they reach out to offer or receive support? Do they stay rather stiffly by your side? Do you have an inclination to reach out, then check it, or pull back?

Our chest area and diaphragm are loaded with information. Once we tune into the breath, we have a reliable monitor of what's going on. The breath is also one of our most valuable tools for shifting what's going on. First, notice your breath right now. Does it feel shallow or deep? Effortless or like you have to work at getting a good breath? Is it rhythmic, or does it have more of a sporadic pattern?

Also with the breath, notice what moves to make room for the influx of air. Does your chest lift up? Do your shoulders move? Do your lower ribs expand? Does your abdomen relax and move out? If you can't tell and would like to know, you can move in front of a mirror and look, you can put your hands on your chest and abdomen, or you can put your hands around your lower ribs.

In my experience as a therapist, I find that people often don't want to tune into their breath. They find it frustrating to pay attention to how they breathe. They might have the sense of doing it wrong or of becoming aware of how difficult it is to breathe naturally and effortlessly. Sometimes they don't feel like they get enough air but don't know what to do about it.

Call on Your Courage

This stage requires courage and fortitude. Because as we become aware and yet we don't have solutions or new patterns to put into place, the awareness can be stressful or even painful. Lots of times we might think we prefer ignorance. But you wouldn't be reading this book if you preferred ignorance—so keep your courage high, get some support, and keep on tracking!

Everyone knows that the gut is a source of information. We don't always know how to interpret the information we get from here, however. For example, when I signed up to go on local TV, my gut was churning so much I thought I'd be sick. I knew it scared me. In this case, I had to decide whether to listen to the fear and not sign up, or to listen to the fear as an indication that I was taking my next big step. This requires some discernment.

So the gut can churn, burn, and tighten. It can flutter with excitement or feel like it's doing somersaults in turmoil. Often, guilt is experienced in the gut as a relentless churning, begging to be relieved. This is one reason we stay stuck in our patterns. Our bodies react when we try to create new patterns, and often it seems the only way to relieve the discomfort is to re-engage the old patterns.

When we think of the body, front and back, we come to the back and spine. We talk about people who have "backbone," meaning they have the strength and fortitude to stand up for themselves (see how many common expressions refer to the body?). When we think about standing tall, we think about owning who we are.

When we "collapse," there's often a folding inward and downward. Our backs or spines can be too rigid, too flexible, have a tendency to take on too much, and so on. Think about your back and what it's telling you. What are your tendencies where your spine is concerned?

Finally we come to our pelvis and legs, the seat of deep emotion and strength. Who has heard, maybe in a yoga class, that we store feelings in our hips? Our hips tighten up and hold on for dear life. It can be difficult to let go here. But for now, we're focused just on noticing. Notice if your legs feel strong, like they can support you. Do you have awareness of your feet? Sometimes fear interrupts our messaging system, and we can lose contact with our legs or feet.

Okay, we've made it through the body, top to bottom. Hopefully by now you have a clearer idea of how much information is available if you choose to tune in. We may not always know what to do with this information, but, for now, we can practice tapping into what's available and ALLOWING what we find.

The other thing about the body's information is that it provides a source of "undeniable knowing." A friend, coach, therapist or mentor can tell you that some particular action is right for you, but it's not the same as accessing your own body sensations, bringing them into awareness, and sorting out what they mean for your next step.

One of the things I like best about doing body work in conjunction with talk therapy is that the weight of the knowing rests inside the person, and not just about what the talking brain has to say. Sometimes our brains can see both sides of things and keep us in perpetual confusion. At those times, tuning into the body's information can be profoundly helpful.

Journal Junction:
Slow Journey Through the Body

Take a moment to write in the space provided in the workbook or in your journal about this experience of becoming more aware by journeying through your body slowly, from head to toe. Write about what was striking or significant to you in doing this exercise. Write about any discoveries you made or any faint awarenesses that became more pronounced or clear.

Up Next . . .

So if building the bridge from our head to our heart (and gut) is what provides us access to our inner wisdom, how do we support that bridge and keep it open and clear for travel? How do we get clear about what we know, feel, and believe?

Chapter 5:
Centering—Getting Clear
about Who You Are

> *At the center of your being you have the answer; you know who you are and you know what you want.*
> —Lao Tzu

In the quest to know what we feel, think, know, and believe, we need to get more acquainted with our inner selves—our *center* if you will. There are various ways to do this, and we'll explore some exercises in the following pages.

Centering with the Breath

Use of the breath as a way to center is perhaps the most time-honored method of centering there is. Meditation practices commonly focus on the breath as a way of slowing down and letting go of distractions. Feeling the breath as it enters is one way to focus sensation in the body; following it as it enters the lungs and the body moves in response is another way.

Various visualization exercises can enhance this experience. For instance, you can imagine an open tube between the nose and the lungs, encouraging the throat to open. You can imagine a light in the belly, which glows when the abdomen relaxes and air enters the lungs. These are some of the numerous ways we can use the breath to center and access our inner selves.

A Centering Exercise
Using Visualization

This is another exercise that promotes an inward focus so again I have created an mp3 for your use. Go to www.NancyJonker.com/MP3 to download the audio version of this exercise if you want to focus on centering without the distraction of reading.

Let's try a centering exercise. Sit in a comfortable chair in a private, quiet place. Put your hand on your *center*, wherever that is for you. This might be over your heart, your solar plexus, or closer to your navel. Close your eyes and visualize your "center." If you've never thought about this before, that's perfectly okay. Just try it and see where it goes.

As you try to be with your center, breathe into the area under your hand. And with your mind's eye, notice whether this center of yours has a shape. If so, what kind? What is the substance? Is it solid, fluid, or something else? Does it have a texture? Is there movement or is it static? Does it have a color? More than one color?

Journal Junction:
Your Center

Notice everything you can about this center of yours. Even if you can't see anything in your mind's eye, write down in your workbook or journal what you noticed. If you had images related to the questions above, describe them. Take some time to describe this experience.

This is an experience that you can come back to as often as you'd like. This is a way for you to begin to explore and own your center. Even if it seemed that there was nothing more there than a black or dark area, it is fertile ground for something to grow and come alive. If you're not intimidated by the experience, try it again in a day or two, or establish a visitation schedule for yourself!

If this was a rich visual experience for you, you can tap into it whenever you'd like. One reason it's so important to connect with our center is that we need a tangible way to connect with our inner knowing, the seat of our own wisdom. We must have a way to access "who we are" if we are going to stand up for ourselves and stand on our own two feet.

One caveat here is that this process often takes courage, fortitude, and persistence. Many times, the first thing people encounter when they do this, especially if they're not typically "centered," is a feeling of sadness. Maybe this is from letting down our guard. Maybe it's about tapping into our deeper selves that don't get enough sway in our day-to-day lives. Whatever the reason, know that sadness often comes when centering, but it paves the way to many good things.

For instance, being in touch with our center is crucial if we're going to maintain good boundaries, be able to remain differentiated in our long-term relationships, and create good energy flow in our bodies and lives. Being centered also fosters our personal power in the dimensions of cognitive and emotional functioning by helping us stay clear-headed, be in tune with our own wisdom, and be able to regulate our emotions.

Visualizing exercises can also be fruitful in allowing ourselves a greater range of behavior, if not in reality, at least in our mind's eye. For instance, you could imagine yourself having a conversation with a friend, partner, or parent. You could imagine saying exactly what you'd like to say and see what that "feels like"—all in your mind's eye.

Journal Junction:
A Conversation in the Mind's Eye

Maybe you want to even write down what you'd like to say and then imagine saying it. Research is showing that doing something in our mind's eye activates some of the same neural pathways as if we were actually doing it. So no need to pick your most difficult conversations, just use it to play with different ways of being and expressing yourself. You'll find space in the complimentary workbook for recording this mind's eye conversation.

Elizabeth, Lady Catherine—and Me

For example, when I was in my early thirties, very intrigued with this whole idea of empowerment and women speaking their minds, I watched the BBC version of *Pride and Prejudice* (1995, with Colin Firth and Jennifer Ehle). I came to the part of Elizabeth's confrontation with Lady Catherine, Mr. Darcy's socially conscious and caustic aunt.

In this confrontation, Lady Catherine insulted Elizabeth and her family one way after another, insults which easily could have triggered Elizabeth's shame and insecurity. Yet at no time did Elizabeth buy into this mindset, fall into shame, or back down!

Elizabeth kept her boundaries clear about what constituted her business versus the business of Lady Catherine. She finally walked away when her self-respect was at stake. In so doing she demonstrated masterly boundary setting and unflappable cognitive and emotional functioning.

I was so impressed and filled with yearning for that ability, I watched that scene dozens of times! Elizabeth Bennett was such a great role model of a strong woman speaking her mind directly to the person who was confronting her, and she was doing it in the moment. What a commanding example of personal power!

As we can see, nourishing our desire and capacity for personal power can happen through various means. Watching and listening to others who possess this skill (even on the movie screen) can provide valuable role models for us to emulate.

Eleanor Roosevelt offered this reminder: "Remember always that you not only have the *right* to be an individual, you have an *obligation* to be one."

Centering—
You and Your Mother's Belly

"When are you going to stop living according to the feelings in your mother's belly?"

This was the question my therapist asked me when I was stewing about a decision regarding my family. I didn't fully comprehend what he was asking, but it felt big.

How do we *not* live according to the feelings in our mother's belly (or partner's or friend's, or father's)? How do we *not* make decisions according to what "sits well" and "doesn't sit well" within us?

How do we know when the guilt and inner churning is a voice to listen to, and when it is calling us back to an earlier way of being (like when our survival really did depend on the good graces of our mother)?

One way to know is to check in with our *center*, our inner knowing. We have to stop the churning long enough to be able to connect, see what we want to do, and give ourselves permission to do it.

Journal Junction:
The Decision Grid

One useful tool for realizing your *center* is called a "decision grid," which I learned from one of my mentors, Darla LeDoux (AlignedEntrepreneurs.com). You can find a decision grid readily presented in the workbook or you can draw one out in your journal. Go to NancyJonker.com/Workbook to download your complimentary workbook.

First determine what it is you are trying to decide.

Then draw two perpendicular lines forming an axis x and y. Then draw two intersecting lines inside so there are four quadrants. At the top of the grid, above the left column write "Love" and above the right column write "Fear." Then label the top row "Yes" and the bottom row "No."

Now go to the first quadrant and write out (it's important to actually write these out) the love-based reasons you would say yes to whatever it is you're trying to decide. Then move to the right column and write down the fear-based reasons you would say yes. Moving to the second row, write down the love-based reasons you would say no, and then the fear-based reasons you would say no.

Your page will look something like this:

What I'm trying to decide:

	Love	Fear
Yes	(Write love-based reasons for saying yes here.)	Write fear-based reasons for saying yes here.)
No	Write love-based reasons for saying no here.)	Write fear-based reasons for saying no here.)

This decision grid is remarkably powerful in helping us see and understand our motivations. We can better evaluate whether fear or self-care is prompting our decision, and then we can move forward accordingly. Even if the fear-based reasons are the strongest and we decide to go with that decision, we do so with greater awareness. This awareness allows us to make choices with increasing freedom, thus increasing our levels of person power in all seven dimensions, as we move through this overall process of understanding ourselves, our motivations, and our choices.

Consulting a Trusted Friend

Another way to discern what to listen to when we're uncertain how to interpret our internal reactions is to run it by a trusted friend or mentor.

Just like that gas gauge that doesn't work properly and needs other sources of data to confirm or deny the validity of what it says, we often need to check in with a steady person or people to help us evaluate.

Getting acquainted with our *center*, the seat of our wisdom and inner knowing, is part of how we become individuals. Staying connected to what we know about ourselves, as Elizabeth did when she was confronted by Lady Catherine is another issue. This requires the skill of *grounding*, or staying connected to what we know and what is real.

Up Next . . .

In the next chapter, we will explore what *grounding* is, how to develop this capacity in ourselves, and how to regain our ground when the proverbial rug gets pulled out from under us.

Chapter 6:
Grounding—Staying Clear about Who You Are

> *Be strong then, and enter into your own body; there you have a solid place for your feet.*
> —Kabir

Maybe we've got the *centering* skill down. When we're quiet and focused, we can have the experience of settling into ourselves. When we do this, we feel like we're *home*. Our heads stop spinning with endless options, and we have a sense of what matters.

Oh, how great it would be to live our lives from this space! But, in the beginning of this journey, most of us don't actually *live* in this space. We visit this space, sort of how a college student might touch base with home.

Grounding is the ability to maintain our connection to this home base even while we're attending to the demands of the day, even while we're connecting with a significant other. How many of us have had the ability to connect with ourselves, but as soon as we connect with someone we really care about, we're more with the other person than we are with ourselves? For women, this is a common experience. We're intuitive, perceptive, and caring. And we can easily lose sight of ourselves.

When I think of grounding, the metaphor of contemporary skyscrapers comes to mind. Not only have engineers changed the construction of these buildings to enable them to withstand the forces of wind and earthquakes, they now insert a tuned mass damper into the core of the building's interior to absorb seismic shock.

There are videos where you can watch the huge gold ball (the tuned mass damper) move as it absorbs the shock. The sway in the skyscraper becomes imperceptible as the counterforce within the core of the building absorbs the impact of the shifting ground. What a model of centering and grounding!

Another great metaphor for grounding is the root system of stately trees. The deeper or wider a tree's roots go into the ground, the better able the tree is to withstand the storms, wind, and drought. Recently I visited the redwood forest in northern

California and learned something about the root system of the redwoods.

These *sequoia sempervirens* have shallow root systems, often going down only five or six feet. Yet their roots can extend over one hundred feet from the base, intertwining with and even fusing with the roots of other redwoods. This powerfully increases their stability during strong winds, rain, and even flooding.

When we want to connect to the ground, to maintain or even regain our center, we are simultaneously needing to connect to our inner selves and the reality of how things currently are. We are seeking to reason without distortions, to test reality quickly and accurately, and in so doing exercise personal power in the cognitive and emotional dimensions.

When we're grounded and connected to our inner wisdom we free up our personal energy and our capacity to take risks. We know we can rely on our inner resilience and thus have little to lose. How do we do this? We dig deep within ourselves, use feedback from trusted others, and challenge ourselves to think clearly about ourselves and our true capabilities. Here's a story to illustrate this.

When I was leading a workshop a few years ago, I was doing so from a depleted state. I had been working against writing deadlines and was preparing until the moment the workshop began. I was co-leading it with the top person in the field who had been my trainer and mentor. There was a strong pull within me to feel small, ill-equipped, and deficient.

Throughout that workshop, I had to dig deep within myself to access my natural intuitive skills, and I had to remind myself, sometimes moment by moment, of the reality that I was competent, skilled, and able to do this work well. I also checked in with my trusted co-leader to support and confirm my view of reality.

Working with myself in this way was a full-time effort, as much as working with the participants in the workshop! In being so purposeful and determined in my quest to ground myself, I confirmed and augmented my person power in the dimensions of my cognitive and emotional functioning, my boundaries, and my capacity for taking risks. In the words of Sheryl Sandberg, "I learned to undistort the distortion."

Being able to stay grounded was critical to my success as a leader. Grounding is critical to all of our success as leaders.

I'm going to take you through some exercises, so you can grow this capacity in yourself and stay connected to your inner wisdom and power on a consistent basis.

Getting Thrown Off-Center

All kinds of things can throw us off-center. To fuel your thinking, here are two categories of challenges that come our way. The first are the *internal* challenges to our inner wisdom. And the second challenge type is *external*, the challenges that come to us through our interactions with others.

The Internal

In terms of internal challenges, we're talking about guilt, shame, anxiety, and insecurity. For example, we might know that it's time to leave a relationship, but as soon as we reach that awareness, our gut begins to churn and our breathing becomes shallow. Guilt and anxiety begin to flood our system as well as words, such as "You can't abandon him," "That's so selfish I can't even go there," or whatever your internal dialogue is.

Or maybe you know it's time to leave your job. And as you contemplate doing so, you get flooded with fears about your ability to find another job or fears about making your business idea work. So maybe you doubt what you know and stay in the land of confusion, where the personal power dimensions of personal energy and cognitive and emotional functioning sit at a low.

Sometimes this confusion feels more like a brain fog. As soon as we see the truth of something, our brain gets cloudy and unable to process. Or we might feel the burning sense of shame.

Shame, you might recall, is distinguished from guilt by how global it is. Guilt is regret or remorse about something we've done: "I've done something bad that I regret." Shame, on the other hand, is regret or remorse about who we are: "I am a bad person" or "I am a worthless human being." These are real examples of our inner self-talk. Shame is debilitating and can take us on a ride like nothing else.

Think back to when you were a little kid and played board games. Remember Chutes and Ladders or CandyLand? Both of these games had the random option of getting sent back—sometimes almost to the beginning of the game. I think about shame as landing on one of those squares that sends you swooshing down the chute back to the beginning. Sometimes it's just a little setback, but sometimes it's a complete ride.

You might be able to call to mind an experience when you were feeling pretty good, then one small thing happened to totally shift your energy. Maybe it was a phone call you got, maybe an email, or some sort of complaint, and it ignited your guilt, shame, or sense of inadequacy. It can feel like getting swooped off your feet (and not in that lovely romantic sense) and getting dumped into a pit.

Journal Junction: Getting Thrown Off-Center from the Inside

Grab your workbook or journal and make some notes about what makes you feel less than who you are. What challenges your certainty about decisions you make, feelings you voice, or skills you have to offer?

The External

The second category of experience that throws us off-center is more relationship-oriented—more external than internal (though, as in the example above, it can trigger the internal challenge as well).

In the workshop I mentioned earlier, there was one person who believed I was not up to snuff, not capable of working with him in the way he wanted. He entered the workshop with the attitude that he was not going to get what he needed from me. This was an external challenge that threatened to trigger my internal slide.

My task became two-fold: stay clear within myself and stay clear with him. That is, not engage in defending myself and not shut down his fears, but allow him to express his needs, wants, and fears while not losing sight of my competence. As far as personal power goes, I had to confirm and really engage with my sense of boundaries and personal energy, and function on high cognitive and emotional levels. Not a small challenge!

Other examples of external challenges to our inner knowing include disagreements with people we want to like us and respect us. Maybe when your coworker, boss, or partner takes a strong position, you no longer know what you believe. Even if you still know what you believe, you may feel entirely unable to speak coherently about it.

Many women I work with tell me about these experiences, and I know them from my own life. It can be hard to articulate our thoughts and positions when faced with conflict and disagreement. We often lose strength in our powers of cognitive and emotional functioning.

One area where external challenges have potentially greater power is relationships with parents (remember my therapist's question—"When are you going to stop living according to the feelings in your mother's belly?"). Because our survival early on truly does depend upon the goodwill of our caregivers, usually our mothers and fathers, we become intensely attuned to what they are feeling. Even as adults, we remain attuned to their feelings.

Let's just take mothers. If your mother invites you to a family gathering that you do not want to attend, how free do you feel to decline? How sensitive are you to her response? Do you have to have a good excuse? Even if you manage to decline, do you feel so much guilt and anxiety afterward that it feels like it would have been easier to attend?

Journal Junction: Getting Thrown Off-Center from the Outside

Take a minute and write some notes about what kinds of external experiences throw you off-center. Get specific about the kinds of conflicts, disagreements, and the people that can really impact your sense of freedom to decide for yourself.

The good news is that there are practical strategies we can use to combat these inner and outer challenges to our staying centered and grounded. Most of us tend to rely on our minds, and we try to talk ourselves into or out of feelings. But because of the triune make-up of our brains, (primitive brain, emotional brain, and cortex), talking ourselves out of guilt, anxiety, or shame is generally not effective and is certainly not efficient.

The techniques that can shift us quickly are body-based practices. We ground through our eyes, hands, and feet—the areas where we contact the outside world. So any exercises that help us engage our eyes, hands, and feet can help us ground. All the grounding exercises I give below you can also find in the free companion workbook.

Practices to Ground Yourself

Modified Mountain Pose

The yoga "mountain pose" is a great grounding exercise. To do a modified version of this pose, plant your feet hip-distance apart and focus on the four "corners" of your feet. Press down the inner ball of your foot, then the outer edge of your foot (while maintaining the first pressure). Add to this by pressing down the inner edge of your heel, then the outside edge of your heel.

Maintain this pressure of all four corners of your feet and feel the muscles in the legs engage. This activates your reaching down into the earth, as opposed to passively standing on the earth. Add to this the "drishti" (focus of the gaze), with hands pressed flat together, level with your sternum, and fingers pointing up, and you've got a serious grounding pose. This modified pose is using the eyes, hands, and feet to ground.

Eyes, Hands, and Feet Grounding Pose

This pose is another great grounding exercise because it engages all three areas that contact the world: the eyes, hands, and feet. To do this pose, stand about a foot and a half away from the wall, legs off-set just a bit.

Place your hands on the wall, fingers spread, and arms straight with elbows almost locked. Then look intently at a spot on the wall in front of you while pushing with your hands and grounding down into your feet. This exercise contains energy in the body (a good antidote when your energy is scattered) and grounds you into the earth at the same time. In this way, it is both a centering and a grounding exercise.

Jumping

Another quick way to get energy down into our legs and feet is to jump up and down in one place. If we wanted to make this even more powerful, we could hold hands with someone and look at them while we jump. This involves the eyes, hands, and feet—the three main areas important for grounding.

High Power Poses

The exciting research in the social psychology field about body language and its ability to shift our chemistry validates these practices and takes them a step further. In a TED talk watched by millions, Amy Cuddy told how spending two minutes in a "high power pose" can increase our confidence hormone and decrease our stress hormone. The opposite is also true. Spending two minutes in a contracted, or "low power pose," increases the stress hormone cortisol and decreases the dominance hormone testosterone.

The implications of this research for you and me are huge! Think about how you sit and move during the day. Are you expansive? Expansive poses are high power poses. Remember Wonder Woman? Her high power pose is standing with legs apart and hands on her hips.

Or think of runners you've seen finishing a race. They're engaging in the universal "victory pose." This is the pose everyone takes when they're proud of an accomplishment or victory (across cultures whether they've seen the pose or not). Arms are in a large V overhead, often with the hands balled into fists pumping the air.

You know those executive chairs that allow the back support to release backward? Imagine sitting back in your chair, interlacing your fingers behind your head, elbows out to the side. This is a high power pose. It's also a high power pose when you keep that posture and put your feet up.

Other high power poses include leaning onto your desk while standing a small distance from it, arms wide, and hands placed expansively forward and wide. One high power pose I like to call the "water cooler" pose is when you find something to lean on with one arm while placing your other hand on your hip. Your legs can be in a separated stance. This one is great because you look casual, but you're actually changing your chemistry while you do it.

It's useful to purposefully engage these poses whenever you need to connect to your power, maybe because you feel small, inadequate, or unsure of yourself. This can be a recovery pose to regain your sense of self and your inner confidence. We'll come back to other ways to recover when we lose our composure or feel our energy and confidence take a downward spiral.

The Ungrounding Impact of Low Power Poses

On the other end of the spectrum are the low power poses. Think about how you might sit while waiting for an interview, waiting to be called into the office. Often we take a really contracted position. Any position that involves folding in and forward can be thought of as a low power pose.

Think about how you sit, walk, and move when you're cold. The shoulders hunch up and in, the belly contracts, and the chest moves forward and down. Maybe you've seen women who cross their legs and hook their foot around their leg. These are ways of becoming small.

The really significant thing about these postures is that they're not neutral. They have an impact beyond what they might communicate to someone else. They communicate something to us. They actually shape who we become.

If I'm a fearful person and often sit in contracted, low power pose ways, I will actually increase my stress hormone and perpetuate the fear cycle.

BUT, if I can interrupt this process through awareness, I can shift into a high power pose and not only not decrease the fear, but shift my chemistry and boost my confidence.

Uses of High Power Poses

This is a game changer!! These poses are available to us pretty much anytime and anywhere. We can do them subtly while in public, or we can take two minutes in a closed conference room, office, or even a bathroom stall.

Imagine being able to access your inner confidence in two minutes! No longer just wishing you could calm down, trying in vain to soothe your nerves. Get into a grounding pose or a high power pose and let your energy shift naturally.

Two occasions come to mind when I used this technique. One, I was getting ready for a radio interview, and I had some waiting time before the interviewer was ready. I found myself sitting with legs crossed and hands on my lap while I reviewed my notes.

Becoming aware of my own body, I stood up and engaged in various high power poses for the next few minutes. By the time the interviewer came to meet me, I was connected to my authentic self and able to speak with confidence.

The other occasion was sitting in a classroom setting. Most of us have had the experience of sitting in a roomful of people and struggling to find our place within the group. In this setting, there were enough people that we needed to raise our hands to speak and to answer questions by show of hands.

There are two ways to raise your hand: the high power pose way and the low power pose way. I realized my tendency was to raise my hand low—with bent arm, my hand about jaw height. This is more typical for females as it turns out. I willed myself to raise my hand high. And in so doing I felt more of a sense of belonging and more confidence in my ability to participate. Hard to believe maybe, but the research is there. Give it a try!

This ability to recover our poise is critical for being able to think on our feet, respond to challenges, and make quick decisions. Who doesn't remember a time when you're clicking along in your day, an email comes in (or a phone call, text, or your boss stops by), and then your energy completely deflates?

Maybe we fall down the shame spiral. Maybe we get angry, but there's nowhere to go with it. Maybe we get anxious and start the endless spinning in our minds. Or, worse yet, maybe we go blank and have no idea what just happened. Maybe we go find some snacks!

When we get derailed like that, we need a way to recover. In the moment, we can try things like meditation or visualizations (to reconnect to our center). Or we could use a grounding technique or a high power pose. Any of these can be helpful in the moment to boost our personal power in our cognitive and emotional functioning, personal energy, and capacity to take risks.

Practices to Regain Grounding and Shift Energy

Recovery from Deflation Practice

For long-term success and to be less susceptible to these energy shifts, we can engage in some practice of these skills.

Journal Junction: What Derails Your Energy? Identifying the Taboos

Here's how the practice works. Grab your workbook or journal, so you can write down some phrases or comments that stop you in your tracks. Let's say, in the personal arena, you've just had a talk with your mother, and she implied you were being selfish.

Maybe now you're stewing about not feeling like a good daughter. But it's more complicated because you really believe that the action you want to take would be good for you. But you find yourself unable to get out of this dilemma of whether you're right and justified to make this decision or you should relent and do what she wants.

In your journal, see if you can get to the "taboo" involved. For the example above, it would be something like "Nice girls aren't selfish." Or "Good daughters don't say no." Or "Being selfish is bad." Notice what you feel when you write these down. Notice what your breath does, what your belly feels, what tenses up, what releases.

The idea behind this "recovery practice" is that you start out grounded. Then you tell yourself a taboo or an injunction such as the examples above. You attune to the impact on your energy—whether it knocks you off-center, whether you feel deflated, whether you feel defeated, whether you feel sad, anxious, or angry. Next you use grounding techniques to shift your energy purposefully. You recover.

Permission Practice

It can also be helpful to give yourself permission to be anxious, sad, or angry, and express it (to your empty room or to a trusted friend who's exploring this exercise with you). You can really dive in, shouting, swearing, and disagreeing. Or you can state things matter-of-factly. The idea is to give yourself a new experience in response to the old message.

This recovery practice is more of a protest against taboos. It involves allowing yourself to experience your full range of feelings in response to the taboos and to express them the way you feel them—in all their variety. This is another way to purposefully shift energy. This is particularly effective to do in a group setting as part of a workshop, but it's possible to use this on your own using your journal or the companion workbook.

Journal Junction:
What Would You Like to Express?
Protesting the Taboos

Once you have identified the taboos (in the previous exercise), you can work with your reactions to them. In the recovery exercise above, your focus was on regaining your ground by shifting your energy and literally finding the ground beneath you. In this exercise, the focus is on moving through the feelings that may block you.

In the workbook, begin by writing what you'd like to express. For the example above, where the taboos were "nice girls aren't selfish" or "good daughters don't say no," you may notice anxiety, guilt, or maybe anger. Maybe you get angry in response to your guilt!

Allow yourself the freedom to express whatever it is you feel, working through the feelings as you express them either in the privacy of your own room or with a trusted friend. Writing and doing allows this new experience to become embedded in your mind and body, creating avenues for change.

Up Next . . .

So we've learned to find our center, discover what this inner wisdom has to say, to stay connected for longer periods of time, and to reconnect as needed through grounding postures and high power poses. Now it's time to think about the container for all of this: our boundary system.

Chapter 7:
Boundaries—Honoring
Who You Are

> *Daring to set boundaries is about having the courage to love ourselves, even when we risk disappointing others.*
> —Brené Brown

As our skin provides a boundary for our muscles, blood vessels, and tissue, our psychological boundary helps us know the limits of who we are (and who we are not). This is a hard concept to articulate because, in some ways, it seems really obvious what our psychological boundaries are; however, in other ways, it seems totally nebulous.

What are psychological boundaries, anyway? We can have boundaries around our time and how we spend it. We have boundaries regarding people, those we'll be with and those we say no to, as well as the level of intimacy we have with different people.

We can have boundaries around different activities—yes, I'll zipline, but, no, I won't bungee jump; or yes, I'll read a book, but, no, I won't go jogging. And of course, we have boundaries around our physical space.

Go back to the exercise in Chapter 4 where you had a friend walk toward you until you told them to stop, the "boundaries and bodily cues" exercise. Our physical, energetic system is constantly giving us messages about what we want, what feels okay, and what stresses our system. Depending on our experiences growing up, we learned to either override these messages or to honor them and listen.

We can think of boundaries and our use of them as occurring on a continuum. If we think of boundaries for a moment like a cloak or second skin, we see that the "fabric" could be full of holes and gaps, or very tightly woven so that not much passes in or out. In this way, then, we can anchor the two ends of the continuum with the idea of a porous boundary on one side and a tightly woven or rigid boundary on the other side.

Our capacity to establish and maintain boundaries falls somewhere on that continuum.

The "Country" Concept

If we further develop this concept of boundaries, we can borrow the metaphor of how a country has both territory and resources to protect. The country may use one of two basic ways to safeguard those resources. If the country has an abundance of soldiers, it may use these soldiers to provide "border patrol" around the perimeter of their territory.

However, if the country doesn't have an abundance of soldiers and knows it can't protect the border adequately, it might pull all its resources into a fort and protect its people and precious possessions in this way.

We can think of our boundary systems as functioning much like that of a country. If we have plenty of resources to protect our border and believe that this will be effective and important, we will guard and defend ourselves at the border. If, however, we feel limited in our resources or don't believe we can be effective or that it's important to defend our border, we may pull our precious resources deep inside and protect them there.

The Developmental Boundary Exercise

Creating a Visible Boundary

I was introduced to this concept when attending a Radix® workshop in Albuquerque, New Mexico.

We did an exercise around boundaries where we took a great deal of time establishing our desired physical boundary. We had a partner from the workshop walk toward us from varying angles, and we would mark on the floor where we wanted them to stop. Then we used string to mark out our territory.

Differing Levels of Development

The next part of this exercise was to experience different levels of developmental abilities. At first, we had no language, just staying in place and only able to make sounds. Next, there was staying in one place, but we were able to make movements of arms and legs (think here how babies can kick with their legs and move their arms even though they're lying in one place). On it goes—being able to make sounds, then saying a word or two, being able to actually move from one place in the circle to another, and eventually being able to use language in phrases and sentences.

Our partners in this exercise were instructed to cross over our boundary, intruding into the space we had established for ourselves. Our job was to protect our boundary as best we could given our developmental ability (we did this multiple times, each round gaining a new developmental capacity).

This exercise completely opened my eyes to a process I had no idea was in place for me. I realized I was relatively indifferent when my partner crossed my boundary. It didn't really seem like my boundary, even though I was the one who had set it up in this elaborate process. I didn't care! And I didn't treat it like a boundary!

Out of the corner of my eye, I could see other people in the room making noise, moving around, conveying to their partners that it was not okay for them to violate their boundaries. But I wasn't doing that. There were some others who weren't doing that as well. I was totally intrigued. What was going on here? Why was I so indifferent when others were clearly invested?

The Big Take-Away on "Border Patrol vs. Fort" Styles

From this experience, I began to learn about the "border patrol versus fort" style of protecting boundaries. People who pull into their fort (usually their head and/or the core of their body) are lackluster about protecting the perimeter. They know there's not enough soldiers to get around and someone can just move a little ways over and get in, so not much effort goes toward protecting the boundary. These are the folks who learned in their early lives that people could intrude on them and there wasn't much they could do about it. So, in a clever countermove, they pulled their energy and resources inside.

But here is the conundrum. This is the phenomenon of doing something to feel safe when it actually puts us more at risk. If I pull into my core and pull my energy out of my muscles and skin so that my "true self" feels safe, I have actually made my physical self more vulnerable.

Perhaps this is you. Perhaps these are people you know and care about. I have observed this to an extreme degree with people.

A Guy in a Bar and My Friend

One time, I was with two friends, one male and one female, at a local restaurant/bar. While there, a guy in the bar came up to my friend and began whispering in her ear. He was trying to coax her into leaving with him. My friend did nothing but smile. She didn't encourage him, didn't say yes, and didn't leave the bar with him. But she did nothing to stop him or tell him to get back. And this was not someone she knew.

When finally this guy left, I asked her how she could stand that. What she said reinforced what I had been learning about boundaries. She said no matter how close he had gotten, he could not get to "her." "She" was locked deep inside where he had no access.

While this might be true, what is also true is that my friend's attitude left her totally vulnerable. She felt safe, and she was confident she wouldn't be going anywhere with him, but she lacked the ability to tell him to back off. And she lacked the will or ability to move herself away from him. Now, maybe she got something from these kinds of exchanges. But as her friend, I know she was troubled by these kinds of interactions every week—sometimes in the workplace, sometimes in social settings, sometimes simply walking down the street.

These kinds of experiences can reinforce a worldview that says people are inappropriate, they feel free to ignore my personal space, I am right to lock away my precious resources deep inside and not worry about the outside because it's impossible to protect anyway.

Guys at a Conference and a Colleague

Another example of this occurred when I was at a residential conference sharing a suite with a woman I didn't know who was also attending the conference. She was a striking woman, beautiful in appearance, soft-spoken, and polite.

Toward the end of the five-day conference, she came into our room and started talking about her experience with men at the conference. One man she had met there dropped off coffee by her door each morning. Other guys made a point of sitting by her for lunch each day. Others walked her to and from her room, acting like they had been friends for a long time.

She expressed her confusion about these interactions and wondered if my roommates and I had experienced this as well. No, we hadn't. This just added to her distress. Why were these people treating her this way? Well, she had asked a group of women who were all in the helping field. We had no shortage of empathy and explanations!

Eventually, I offered her this very framework for understanding boundaries. I explained it, then asked her if it made any sense, though I didn't need to ask because all along she had been nodding and responding like a big light bulb had just gone on in her head. She had never heard this framework before but it made total sense to her. She got how she was giving off signals in her interactions with others and how they in turn interacted with her, even though this was all below her level of awareness.

The next day she told me she spent more time reflecting and thinking that night than sleeping. She could see how she was leaving herself vulnerable in her efforts to feel safe and to feel a sense of belonging. She decided she was going to seek out a coach or therapist to help her with this blind spot, so she could both feel safe and actually be safer in the world. So she could feel a sense of belonging, without having to give up her personal space.

Becca's Story: Rigid Border Control

An example of someone with a boundary style more on the rigid side of the continuum is Becca. Becca came to see me because she was dissatisfied in her relationship with her partner. They were not close, they often bickered, and she felt alone much of the time.

Becca worked in a large accounting firm, and she had her desired level of responsibility there. But she seldom felt satisfied. She felt left out from the different groups of women there, even to the point of wondering whether they were talking about her or laughing at her. She did her work well though she was often in pain from the tension in her muscles. She found it hard to relax once she got home and often consumed two glasses of wine just to be able to de-stress.

In our work together, Becca often had trouble answering questions about how she was feeling. The only feeling that was readily and consistently available to her was the experience of self-pity. By her own acknowledgement, this wasn't all that helpful to her, and she typically felt a void inside. Intimate connections with her partner were hard to establish because each of them had trouble communicating heart to heart.

The work with Becca was around helping her develop easier access to her feelings and to her center of inner wisdom. She lived relatively cut off from the tender feelings in her heart, so our work was around reconnecting to those and opening the pathway through the throat and neck between her head and heart. As she did this, her life and relationships began to open up in new and satisfying ways.

Journal Junction: Identifying Your Boundary Style

Below are ten questions to help you determine whether you use the fort style of boundaries. Maybe you already know your style because you see yourself in the example of one of these women. But, if not, use the workbook or your journal to answer these questions. Feel free to elaborate and write some stories of your experiences, so you come to understand how this process takes place in you.

1. Do strangers act like they know you and treat you like you're their good buddy even if you've just met?
2. Do friends and acquaintances think they know you really well, yet you feel like they don't know you much at all?
3. Do you wonder why patterns such as these keep repeating?
4. Do you feel tightness in your chest and gut when someone bothers you or you feel threatened?
5. Do you ever or often lose awareness of your feet or legs?
6. Do you get dizzy and feel like your head might float away?
7. Is it hard for you to say no and mean it?
8. Do you find yourself wishing for more space but not asking for it?
9. Do you often feel depleted or exhausted?
10. Do you believe that no matter how close someone gets physically they "can't get to you"?

If your answer to the above questions tended to be yes, you are probably more on the fort style side of the continuum of boundaries (which is on the porous side of that psychological skin or cloak).

If your answers were more often negative, read on. The following questions are to help identify boundaries on the more rigid side of the continuum. Again, writing beyond a yes or no can be helpful to your understanding of how you use boundary strategies in your day to day life. Because most of us learn our lessons early on and all too well, they become so automatic we often don't even notice what we're doing.

1. Do you find that it's hard to "let people in"?
2. Do you wish for more involvement with others but don't know how to bring it about?
3. Do you tend to have tight muscles and reddish skin?
4. Do you often feel left out of the group?
5. Do you find it hard to have heart to heart connections with people you care about?
6. Do you often feel "unseen" by people you want to be involved with?
7. Is it hard for you to access or talk about your feelings?

If your answers were positive in this second group of questions, you may be more on the "armored" side of the boundary continuum. For you the challenge is not to establish and maintain boundaries as much as it is to soften them and become more flexible.

If this exercise seemed confusing to you, don't worry. Our boundary system isn't a clear-cut system that is easily defined. You may notice that with certain people you behave one way, while with others you behave differently. This exercise is simply to help you become aware of patterns and ways we have of protecting our personal space, our energy, and our resources. Once we become aware, we can develop more choice.

Where Is Your Drawbridge?
The Art of Flexible Boundaries

When we think about healthy boundaries, it's helpful to use the metaphor of a drawbridge. If your castle is on one side of the moat and the people who want to visit you are on the other side, you're going to need a well-functioning and well-oiled drawbridge to invite them into your castle when you want them there. This implies that you have choice in the matter about whom to let in and when, and whom to keep out.

This metaphor also implies flexibility, so that this drawbridge can open and close in accordance with your wishes. The drawbridge would be of little use to you if it were stuck open or closed. But that's exactly how underdeveloped boundaries work when they're either too rigid (keeping everyone out) or too porous (letting everyone in). The only way a drawbridge is useful is if it can open and close upon the command of the operator in the castle.

So what interferes with the functioning of our drawbridge?

This is where the feelings of guilt, shame, and insecurity come into play. When we feel too guilty about setting boundaries or saying no, our system can get overwhelmed and "cave in." Maybe we give too much of our time and energy away just so that we don't have to bear the guilt of saying no.

We can see how being limited in personal power on the emotional functioning dimension is often connected to having limited personal energy, troubles setting and maintaining boundaries, and limited financial freedom.

If we think of a bell curve as it relates to boundaries, at the peak of the curve stand functional, flexible boundaries. In this area, we say yes or no to people, activities, and tasks dependent upon whatever makes sense to us at the time. We can say yes, no, or let me think about it. We don't have to feel guilty, and we can give ourselves permission to want some people close and keep others at a distance.

When our boundaries are too rigid and automatic, we can't decide on a case-by-case basis. That's when our boundaries become a "one-size-fits-all" kind of armor. We don't believe we can afford to let people in, so we keep our boundaries tight and our default answer is no.

In essence, our drawbridge is stuck in the closed position. As we can see, the result of this is gradual isolation. On a smaller scale, rigid boundaries create barriers to intimacy, preventing us from being seen and understood, even when that's what we really want.

Remember Jim Carey in *Yes Man*? At first, he only said no to opportunities and was getting more and more out of touch with his friends. After an intervention at the "Yes Man" conference, he only said yes. Toward the end of the movie we watch him learn the art of a flexible, discriminating boundary.

When our boundaries are too porous, we have a tendency to feel depleted, overwhelmed, and resentful. We give virtually everything we have away—our time, our energy, our talents. In this case, the drawbridge is stuck in the open position and anyone can come and go, taking what they need. Even when we want to pull the drawbridge up, if we haven't worked through feelings of guilt and shame, we won't make those hard decisions because we're convinced we'll feel bad if we say no.

The most extreme kind of porous boundary is when the energy is pulled into the core and out of the periphery all together. In this fort style, there's no point in saying no, you just find alternative ways around the problems. The use of personal power in the dimensions of emotional functioning and personal energy is very low.

Maybe you get sick, so you don't have to go to an event. Maybe you avoid being around at certain times, so the issue of attending never comes up. Maybe you change jobs if someone is bothering you in your current one. Maybe you just put up with a lack of personal space because you're convinced you're not going to get it.

The fort style of boundaries is the most extreme of the porous boundary because it leaves us vulnerable. Particularly if we don't KNOW we're locked up in our fort and leaving the border unattended, we are vulnerable. I've talked with many women who will say things like, "It's okay, there's no way they can get to me. My real self is way in here" (while they point to their heart or solar plexus).

Even though they say this, they have little awareness of what this means for them in terms of their safety in the world. They don't always realize they have abandoned their borders—the perimeters of their personal space. I certainly hadn't realized the extent to which I was indifferent about protecting the boundaries I had set up until that critical exercise. Following that insight, it became my mission to understand boundaries, people's sense of control over them, and their ability to establish and maintain them.

No matter where you are on the spectrum of personal boundaries, there is something to learn. If you're on the rigid side and find you want more connection in your life, you can work with your boundaries to become more flexible. You still have the capability to keep people out when you want (you have that skill down pat), but you'll add the ability to invite people in as well.

If you're on the more porous side, you'll be able to learn how to fill in the holes in your boundary system, so that you have more control and more choice about who gets in and who stays out. You'll also have more choice about where your energy and time goes.

And if you're locked in your fort deep inside your person, you'll learn ways to come out to the border. This is often a gradual process because women don't always feel safe leaving the fort and fully inhabiting their bodies.

Playing with Oppositions

One of the things I do in my group workshops is an exercise called "oppositions." I line up folks across from each other and give them a word or phrase to say. For example, those on the left say, "No," and those on the right say, "Yes." Back and forth they go, saying it softly, matter-of-factly, and later shouting it and stomping their feet. The purpose of this is to give people an experience saying or doing something they would not or could not do in real life.

In this same exercise, I move on to phrases such as "You will" and "I won't." We can explore any theme with this exercise. For example, if we want to explore people's ability to say no to someone in need, I might have one group say, "Please help me," and the other side responds with "Help yourself."

Many women (and men too) would be mortified to say something like that for real, but the experience helps open up something in people that they've previously been closed to. The exercise can give them permission to say something they maybe secretly think or even want to say though they never would.

In this way, people can have the experience of a broader use of personal power in the emotional realm, in the personal energy dimension, and along the boundaries dimension. Having a different reference point can create avenues for change in how we live day to day.

Repetition Compulsion as Expressed in the Body

One of the things we learn when we try new things is that our physiology—our bellies in particular—have a huge pull in keeping our patterns the same. You'll know what I mean if you ever recall a time when you tried saying no to someone (a boss, a spouse, a parent, a sibling) and you got such an active churning in your gut that you were compelled to call them back or go after them to "rectify" the situation.

There's a term in psychology called the "repetition compulsion." The idea behind this is we continue to put ourselves in a similar situation that we found ourselves growing up in in an effort to recycle and eventually correct the pattern. Hence the repetition part.

But the compulsion is the really interesting part. Compulsion is very body-oriented. Think addiction. We get a "fix" by undoing that which makes us feel guilty. We can hardly stand the feeling in our gut when we take a stand with our spouse and have to wait for him to approach us rather than us apologize to him (or whatever the pattern is). We have such an urge to go back and repeat our status quo pattern that we can hardly stand it.

I remember being at a conference with my husband where this exact thing occurred. I made a request of him, and he declined. This was no small request and no neutral response. It felt to me that the health of our relationship depended upon what I had asked. He said no; I pushed the issue to the point that I left for the day, angry, disappointed, and the conflict unresolved.

For the next several hours, I endured crippling rumination and gut churning. I was convinced I was asking too much, that I should not put these kinds of demands on him, that I should go back, apologize, and tell him it was okay.

Needless to say, this is not how change happens! If I had done that, I would have perpetuated the status quo in our relationship. It was agonizing to act differently, but without enduring those hours of confusion and distress, I would not have changed a thing.

This is why so many people have trouble changing their boundaries and asking for what they want or need. Our internal gauge of what's okay screams at us that what we've just done is not okay. Our bodies churn and stay unsettled, convincing us we need to apologize, conform, withdraw our request, or say yes to what we just said no to.

Most people are unprepared for this bodily response when they try to change their behavior. If we're not aware of what's coming, it's easy to misinterpret the signs and tell ourselves we'd better "behave right" and go fix what we did.

So you might be realizing at this point that changing boundaries is challenging. And it involves the body and effective self-talk. If we tell ourselves the same old story, we will not find our way out of our old patterns.

The good news is that there are lots of ways to work with ourselves to create the kind of life and the freedom we want, and to develop increased personal power along several of the various dimensions.

Communicating Boundaries

So how do we communicate our boundaries? How do people know whether we want them to stay away or get close?

Remember that exercise I call "boundaries and bodily cues?" Remember that most of our internal signals are body based? Like our eyes drawing back or tightening up, our chest tightening, or our breathing becoming more shallow or fixed. Maybe our jaw tightens and our throat closes.

An astute observer might notice these things and, if so inclined to behave according to our wishes, back off. But most people aren't that consciously aware of these signals. Plus, we don't want to leave this to chance. We want to communicate our boundaries—our preferences and choices about who comes close and just how close—clearly and unequivocally.

One of the interesting things I've found when doing the "developmental boundary" exercise is that many women, when instructed to use only a word or two, are more powerful and clear than when they have more "resources" available.

For instance, women who said things like "No" or "Back off" were unambiguous in their meaning and intent. But when able to use full sentences, these messages often got lost in politeness and civility. "No!" changed to "I don't want you that close" and "Back off!" changed to "Would you move back please?"

These are fascinating changes. And they teach us something important about the lessons women learn about power and the permission we feel or don't feel about setting and protecting our boundaries.

Once we feel permission to set boundaries and protect them, we can use anything available to help us communicate them. For instance, we can say no with our eyes. Try this now. Lift your eyebrows high into the forehead and say no. Then try to harden your eyes. You can do this by frowning a bit and bringing tension to your eyes as though you're trying to read something you can't quite make out. Now try saying no and see if it's any different.

If you're like most, the second way feels more effective. Eyes that are hardened or "uninviting" are more congruent with saying no than eyes that are wide open. Open eyes tend to be expressions of warmth and invitation, and extremely wide open eyes tend to communicate fear, alarm, or surprise. When one part of our body says one thing and another part says something completely different, viewers are left to make up their own minds.

If you actually try to have your eyes say one thing while your words say another, you'll probably find it's kind of hard to do. I've run workshop exercises where we purposely try to be incongruent. And it's not easy to do. Yet many of us do it unconsciously very easily!

Awareness is key. Feedback is important in developing that awareness because many of us never realize what mixed messages we're giving off. Getting ourselves aligned with one decision, one message to convey, is the first step. Next is making sure that our bodies support what we're saying. "Body" here includes the eyes, voice, shoulders, arms, hands, torsos, as well as legs and feet.

"How could our shoulders have a part in this?" you ask. Well, imagine yourself making a strong statement to someone about your political beliefs. Then, at the end of it, you shrug your shoulders just a bit. The shoulder shrug could be saying something like "Well, that's just how I see it," "You may not like what I just said," or "For whatever that's worth." Sometimes we add those words, but even when we don't say them, our bodies can say them for us—with or without our knowing it.

We do other little things like that to diminish our message or take it away. We might tilt our head to the side as in "What do I know?" or again "That's just how I see it." This might even be coupled with a shrug. Sometimes these are friendly little gestures meant to say, "I mean no harm, I'm not trying to take you on." But sometimes they rob us of our power.

Working with Boundaries in the Body

As with grounding, so with boundaries. Grounding helps us redistribute energy that is caught up in our heads or deep in our cores, sending it back down into the power of the hips, legs, and feet. When we're working directly with boundaries, it is all about getting the energy out to the edges of ourselves—the periphery of our bodies, such as the muscles in our arms and legs. Some people feel tingling all along their arms when they do this.

Bringing our energy into the periphery of our bodies is one reason weightlifting can be helpful. If we think of our muscles and skin as the container for our tissue, blood vessels, and organs, it makes sense that we need a strong container.

Psychologically we need a strong container too. Because of the unity of body and mind, having a strong physical container can help us have a strong psychological boundary so long as we stay aware of what we are doing and why.

Depending on where we land on the continuum of boundaries, we'll work with boundaries a little differently. If we are overly protective of our boundary, too vigilant about letting people in so that we suffer from isolation, the issue is about softening the boundary, not strengthening it.

Instead of hardening the eyes and sending more energy outward, we would work to soften the eyes, allowing ourselves to be seen. This can be a scary prospect when much of our energy has been to keep people out and to keep ourselves hidden.

When we are on the more rigid side of the boundary continuum, it can be hard for us to center. So not only do we keep ourselves hidden from others, we may actually be hidden from ourselves. The centering exercises in the earlier chapter may be really important, but really hard to do!

When so much of our energy gets directed outward and is contained in the muscles and skin, we may not have easy access to our feelings. So part of the work for those of us on this side of the continuum is to spend more time centering and visualizing our inner life.

One more aspect of softening rigid boundaries is using our voice to invite. When we want the full range available to us—to be able to keep people out when that's appropriate and to be able to invite them in when that's what we want—we have to work with each area of the body and each mode of expression to develop that range. So with the voice, we want to be able to be loud and unambiguous, but also to be soft and inviting.

This concept of range is a critical concept for being able to have choice and options in our life. We don't want to be stuck on one end of the continuum or stuck with just one way of being in the world. We want to be able to function with high levels of personal power across the seven dimensions, including here emotional functioning, boundaries, personal energy, and relationship quality.

Up Next . . .

We now have a clear idea of the importance of boundaries for our overall healthy functioning, and we understand the difference between the border patrol versus fort style of boundaries. We have seen how rigid boundaries can result in gradual isolation and how extremely porous boundaries can leave us depleted and even at risk.

The drawbridge analogy helps us understand the art of flexible boundaries. We discussed ways of communicating boundaries with our eyes, voice, and posture, as well as ways of developing more flexible boundaries through new ways of interacting. Next we move into my POWER formula for increasing personal power in every aspect of our lives.

Chapter 8:
My POWER Formula—
How to Increase Your
Personal Power

> *Good for the body is the work of the body,*
> *good for the soul the work of the soul, and*
> *good for either the work of the other.*
> —Henry David Thoreau

For all of us who want to be more empowered but aren't exactly sure how to get there, I developed the **POWER formula**, a simple acronym to help us learn and remember how we can have more efficacy and impact.

P—Permission

We begin with *permission*. We give ourselves *permission* to be ourselves, to have power, to set boundaries, and to be selfish. We give ourselves *permission* to tend to our health, to practice exquisite self-care, to honor who we are inside.

We give ourselves *permission* to be bold, unapologetic, and courageous. We give ourselves *permission* to be compassionate toward ourselves. And we claim both the privilege and obligation of being fully ourselves.

Until we give ourselves *permission*, we cannot live in accordance with our full power. Power is not something simply gifted to us; it is something we need to nurture and cultivate. Giving ourselves *permission* to develop our personal power along the seven dimensions, and to live out of that power, sets us on the road to being our best selves.

Permission is not always the easiest thing to grant. Sometimes those pesky beliefs creep in about ambition, selfishness, and strength. We need a framework for holding these new ideas in our minds and hearts.

Have you ever heard the expression, "Have a strong back and a soft front?" This is a concept developed by Joan Halifax, author of *Being with Dying: Cultivating Compassion and Fearlessness in the Presence of Death*. She writes about the importance of developing a strong spine that helps us face the demands of life. We need a sturdy backbone to stand up for what we believe and to stand tall under the weight of ordinary and extraordinary challenges that come our way.

In addition to our strength, however, we need softness. We need an open, compassionate heart that pulsates with grief, joy, sadness, pain, happiness, and gratitude. A softness that invites people to us and showers them with compassion.

Either of these by themselves wouldn't survive. A strong backbone all alone becomes rigid and susceptible to hardness and eventual collapse. A soft heart by itself might bleed out, get squashed, or become overwhelmed by the weight and shifting of feelings.

One of the things I like best about yoga is its balanced emphasis on strength and flexibility. For many women, we confuse strength with rigidness or overuse of power. When we aim to be strong, we might fear that we'll lose our softness and approachability. Approachability without the strength can make us doormats, and strength without the softness makes us lose some of our best qualities as women. So let's marry the two, just as yoga does.

In the original *Star Trek* television series, there is an episode called, "The Enemy Within" which vividly portrays this truth. For those of you who are familiar with the series, here's the recap. The transporter system is down, unusable, because it has split its users into two halves. First a dog and now Captain Kirk have been split into two. One "personality" is docile, kind, gentle and indecisive. The other "personality" is conniving, manipulative, aggressive, and power-hungry.

In this episode, crew members are trapped on a planet, and temperatures down there are dropping so low the crew will not be able to survive for long. But they cannot be transported back to the Enterprise without being killed or damaged in the process because of the problems with the transporter. Kirk has to deal with this crisis with a very tight deadline (nothing he's not done before, but now he is functioning with only half of his faculties).

We see the "good" Kirk almost undone by his compassion for his crew. He cannot make a decision or plan. Meanwhile the "evil" Kirk is being aggressive with a female crew member, as well as trying to get control of the ship.

In one memorable scene, gentle Kirk realizes he cannot function without his other half. Even though he is afraid of and disgusted by the behavior of the other Kirk, he realizes he needs him—they both need each other to function effectively and compassionately in his role as captain.

So it is with us. We need aggression, sometimes to ward off people who would take advantage of us. We need our wits about us. We need to look out for ourselves. We are allowed to be selfish as well as compassionate.

We are allowed to nourish ourselves with good food, to make time for exercise, to arrange our lives so we can get adequate and nourishing sleep. We are allowed to get massages and to socialize with friends. We are allowed to have personal power and to exercise it along all seven dimensions. We are allowed because WE give ourselves *permission*.

O — Observation

We also need to *observe* ourselves and how we're relating and functioning in our lives. Remember, self-awareness follows body awareness. We need to tune in and develop an attitude of curiosity. We need to *observe* and allow without judgment.

Change is a process. It occurs in increments and approximations. Journal writing can be helpful in this process because it helps us track what we're working on and the progress we're making. We can keep a journal to develop our attunement and to practice non-judgment and awareness.

What is it that we need to *observe*?

We can *observe* our physical reactions to people, to invitations, to requests, to job demands, etc. We can *observe* our repetitions—those conflicts with people or around situations that we find ourselves in again and again.

We can *observe* and write about our strong urge (compulsions) to fix problems and to maintain the status quo. We can *observe* our guilt, shame, and insecurity, noticing whether they're running the show or whether we're willing and able to tolerate the feelings, so that our inner wisdom directs our decisions and behaviors.

We can *observe* how we talk to ourselves. Not only the things we say to ourselves, but the tone of our inner voice. We need to listen for acceptance and encouragement versus judgment and criticism.

Many of us feel that we need that "kick in the pants" to get us off the couch, to keep us moving. When I ask women what their fear is if they stop being so hard on themselves, more often than not their answer is they're afraid they'll become a couch potato.

Most of us have had the experience of being judged, shamed, or prodded into performance. Maybe this approach even improved our performance. But most of us have also had the experience of being inspired by someone—maybe a teacher or coach. Take a minute and compare the impact of being criticized into good performance versus inspired into doing your best. It is a myth that we need criticism and kicks to get us motivated.

Effective Self-Talk

Recent research on self-talk suggests that many of us talk to ourselves in ways that reinforce negative habits and behavior. We tell ourselves we're idiots. We berate ourselves for what we just said. We tell ourselves we're worthless. And we say all these things in critical, condemning tones (even in our mind's ear).

Far better self-talk starts with us calling ourselves by name. Fascinating research suggests that we are far wiser when we talk to ourselves using our name rather than using "I." It actually activates different parts of our brain. And, as most of us already know, we are much kinder to our friends than we are to ourselves. We make allowances for our friends' mistakes and mishaps. But we are unforgiving when it comes to ourselves.

No more! Decide to treat yourself as well as you would treat a friend. Talk to yourself as lovingly as you would a friend. Treat yourself with as much respect as you would a friend.

In her research on self-esteem and self-compassion, Kristin Neff has found that the quest for self-esteem can be as negative for us as the lack of it! Self-esteem often depends on rating ourselves as special or above average. It is based on a comparison model, and the resulting sense of self-worth is often contingent upon these comparisons.

Rather than pursuing self-esteem, we would do better to cultivate compassion. Precisely when self-esteem lets us down, like when we receive evidence that we're not in fact above average, compassion can be the balm for our hurting soul. Compassion creates a loving, connected presence that allows us to withstand the hardships of life.

On Self-Compassion

Self-compassion has three parts. It begins with an attitude of *kindness toward ourselves*. Here we need to counter our inner critic and all that our critic wants for us but goes about getting in the wrong way. We can be kind, we can check in with ourselves and see whether we're okay (rather than jump right into problem-solving mode). We can offer understanding about the disappointments we face.

The second part of self-compassion is *common humanity* or what I call *taking our part in the circle of life*. Life's challenges can make us feel isolated. We are quick to use our experiences to cut ourselves off from others.

This second component of self-compassion is all about using a particular hardship as a vehicle to connect with others. For example, let's say you're having a difficult time getting your boss to listen to you. You make an effort, but he comes down hard on you. You feel embarrassed and on the edge of shame.

And then you recognize that this is a hard moment—you offer yourself a little kindness and then think about all the women like you who struggle to be heard in the workplace. You remind yourself that this is a common dilemma (as opposed to "OMG, I can't believe that just happened! I just got called out in front of everyone! Why do these things always happen to ME?").

This example brings up the third aspect of self-compassion, which is *mindfulness*. This relates directly to the cognitive functioning dimension of personal power. Being mindful about the challenges we face means neither minimizing nor catastrophizing. Oddly enough, we tend to do one or the other.

We may not pause long enough to let the difficult situation register and, thus, minimize the challenge we're facing. Or, we tend to blow it out of proportion (because of our strong feelings about it and our own insecurities) and make it worse than it is in reality.

Mindfulness is a practice, not only as applied to self-compassion, but in its own right. To be mindful in the moment is one form of being both centered and grounded at the same time. We can access our feelings about what is happening, but we also stay connected to what is real, not letting our thinking slide out of control or negating the impact of what we're facing.

One useful idea here is to visit the self-compassion.org website and take the "Self-Compassion Assessment." The value of this assessment isn't just to give you an idea of your overall capacity to be self-compassionate. The results of this assessment also break down your tendencies along the various components of self-compassion, helping you see where the weak points are that you can address.

For example, when I took the self-compassion assessment, I learned that though I was pretty good at accepting my mistakes and giving myself compassion at those times, my greatest challenge was *recognizing* when I was experiencing a hard time. Without registering the hard time, it's hard to apply the self-compassion. We don't even "know" that we need it.

Again, using the complimentary workbook or a journal to track some of this can be so helpful. There are numerous exercises available that foster the development of self-compassion, including writing a compassionate letter to yourself for seven days. The effects of these practices are very robust in developing and maintaining increased life satisfaction.

Research has also shown that writing your way through problems and feelings can be very effective. In fact, writing for 20 minutes a day for at least four days in a row prompted 40% fewer doctor's visits, as reported by James Pennebaker in *Expressive Writing: Words that Heal.*

So in *observing* our attitudes, our inclination to judge ourselves, our inner conflicts and our hopes for freer living, we lay the groundwork for living with more personal power. Our thinking gets clearer, our emotions come into focus, and we begin to track and channel our personal energy.

We can *observe* how we manage our drawbridge, and with this awareness, develop more options for ourselves. When we *observe* our relationship patterns, and the things that trip us up, we lay the groundwork for developing new patterns and ways of being with those we love.

When we *observe* our behavior and attitudes around finances, we set the stage for powerful change in this aspect of our lives. We begin to become more informed and more invested, which can lead to more powerful living and more financial freedom.

And finally, when we *observe* our fears, our responses to mistakes, and our capacity to settle ourselves, we increase that all-important skill of resiliency. When we trust ourselves to bounce back from challenges, "failures," and disappointments, we can allow ourselves to take more risks.

W—Wonder Woman

After *observing* our own process and what it is that drives us, we can *wonder*. We can foster that attitude of curiosity and non-judgment.

And we can call upon *Wonder* Woman! *Wonder* Woman's famous stance is one terrific example of a high power pose that we can use to regulate our hormones, boosting our confidence and decreasing our stress.

When we can be *expansive*, when we can take up space in the room and move our energy all the way out to the edges of our body, we have already increased our empowerment. Whatever we do next will be a more confident, efficacious act because we will be calling forth and acting upon the impulses of our true selves.

Remember that these high power poses can be done in private for two minutes prior to a challenging event or can be unobtrusively engaged in while talking or presenting. Be like *Wonder* Woman and be expansive!

E—Expand into Your Body, into Your Life, and into Your Strengths

The first thing to do when *expanding* into our strengths is, ironically, to embrace our imperfections. The quest to be perfect and to ward off feelings of hurt, possible rejection, and loneliness puts us on a road to isolation and frustration.

It's a hard lesson to learn that vulnerability is part and parcel of strength. We are powerful when we can be authentic and have nothing to hide. We can have open hearts and a strong backbone.

Part of embracing our imperfections is forgiving ourselves for not knowing the answers, for making mistakes, and for not being as far along as we wish we were. In accepting where we are, we open up to new possibilities. We can form new opinions of ourselves, steeped in compassion.

For many of us, this begins to sound too "soft." "That's not how we get strong," you might say! You might even think that forgiving, accepting our imperfections, and surrounding ourselves with compassion isn't the way to be strong!

And yet it is.

Quoting from Joan Halifax again: "Don't ever think compassion is weak. Compassion is about strength."

Let me reiterate here. When we can show compassion to ourselves, we can actually take more risks. We can take more risks because less is at stake. Our whole opinion of ourselves isn't on the line. We can take more risks, be more open, and recover more easily from "failures." Compassion enhances our personal power.

Our personal power is also enhanced by focusing on our strengths. Being trained as a clinical psychologist, I was taught to assess and diagnose people's pathology. Basically, I was taught to figure out what was wrong with them. In my twenty-five years of working with people, I have come to realize that it is far more effective to work with people's strengths.

Many of us don't really know our strengths. We tell ourselves whatever story we believe about ourselves and often don't open up to people's feedback about our strengths—often it is what they love and appreciate about us. Because our talents tend to be what we do naturally, it's easy to overlook or discount them. "Doesn't everyone do that?"

It's also easy to get preoccupied with our perceived weaknesses and what we want to improve in ourselves. Most of us believe this is the way to greatest success. But research has shown that when we focus on what's working already and try to enhance those things, we are far more effective than when we focus on the problems. This can be a difficult shift to make!

The 25's Top 3

In order to enhance our strengths, we need to know what they are. Not so long ago, I had the assignment of asking 25 people what they thought my three greatest strengths were. My first impulse was just to skip this assignment. Who wants to go around asking that?

But I knew there was value in this if I could find a way to do it. So I did. I emailed 25 people and asked them what they thought my top three strengths were. I was tempted to give them multiple choice or provide some kind of template to make the task easier. But I didn't. I left it open-ended.

There was remarkable consistency in their responses. What an amazing experience! People were happy to participate in my assignment and seemed to have no trouble coming up with their answers. And it allowed me to see myself the way others see me. I actually had a spreadsheet with their responses and could categorize them and discern my top strengths as others saw me.

Your Turn with the 25's Top 3

I would not have done this exercise if it had not been assigned. And I would have missed out on great information. So that's why I'm including this assignment here and in the complimentary workbook. Find a way to ask 25 people what they see as your top three strengths. I recommend email because you can actually set it up as a survey and have their responses come back into a spreadsheet. But however you do it, take the risk and ask. Use this assignment to discover something amazing.

StrengthsFinder 2.0 Profile

Another way to discover your strengths is to take a strength-based assessment. The StrengthsFinder Profile was developed by Gallup to help people spend less time trying to correct their weaknesses and more time enhancing their strengths. Through research with millions of people, they parsed out 34 distinct themes of talent.

Now Gallup offers sophisticated reports about the talent themes, complete with action guides about how to develop them into strengths. They also provide a more customized report about how the top five signature themes for any given person work together and create a coherent whole. These Strengths Insights convey how you stand out from among the rest.

So your second assignment is to take the StrengthsFinder 2.0. Then read the reports, record your findings in your workbook or journal, and share your results. Put your top five strengths on your bathroom mirror, on your computer screen, behind your desk, or on your phone—somewhere you'll see often. Let yourself reflect on and absorb your strengths as you begin to own them and grow into them. There is no substitute for this, so be sure to do it!

Kolbe Index

Another powerful strengths assessment is the Kolbe A™ Index. The Kolbe Index measures "conation"—the third aspect of the mind. We all have an instinctive way that we go about accomplishing tasks and goals. Whether we need to gather facts, improvise, follow procedures, or use our hands to implement change, we each have an instinctive style, and that's what "conation" refers to.

Many of us don't know anything about our instinctive style. I had been a psychologist for twenty-six years before I heard of conation! For me, taking the Kolbe Index answered the question of whether I was lazy. If you put me in a room full of dishes that need to be washed and food put away, I'd just as soon walk out of the room and buy new dishes as begin to sort and clean.

I also don't like to garden, weed, or do yard work. I don't like to change lightbulbs and may endure a dark room for weeks before I put in a new bulb. For the longest time, I thought I was lazy. Unwilling. But that didn't make sense with other patterns in my life. I was told more than once that lazy people don't get PhDs. Lazy people don't start businesses. But I wasn't sure. Until I took the Kolbe Index, I didn't understand how these patterns fit together.

The Kolbe Index measures an enduring style of being in the world. Kathy Kolbe, the author and designer of the assessment tool, refined the theory of conation following a car accident that impaired her cognitive functioning and sent her emotional regulation system on a roller coaster.

Over time, she realized that though her thinking capacity was altered and her emotions were all over the place, her way of approaching problems and goal-directed behavior was the same as it had been over her whole life. So she studied this and through careful psychometric work was able to develop an assessment that reliably measures these clusters of behavior derived from the instinctive nature of each person.

It matters a lot that the Kolbe Index is strengths based. In the report that follows the assessment,

Kathy Kolbe's voice comes on as she talks about what a wonderful combination this particular modus operandi is. When we become aware of our instinctive style of solving problems and going after goals, it adds to our ability to function effectively on our own and within a team.

This increases our personal power in the areas of cognitive and emotional functioning, personal energy, boundaries, and quality of relationships. Many conflicts within a team or in a relationship can be traced to differences in these instinctive styles. Working with our strengths can also increase our power in the financial realm.

If you want to become more self-aware and have more knowledge about your strengths and how to work in ways that naturally rely on them, go take the Kolbe Index assessment. In the complimentary workbook, there is a section for you to explore and record your findings and insights from this assessment.

There are other packages available on the Kolbe website (www.kolbe.com) as well, so employers can see how well their expectations match up with their employees' MO, expectations within a relationship, and information about how we would tackle different professions and jobs. But if you just want to get started, take the Kolbe A and learn about yourself and your style of striving. Then accept what you learn, embrace your MO, and *expand* into your strengths!

100% Responsibility

Another aspect of *expanding* into our life and our strengths is to take FULL RESPONSIBILITY for ourselves—100% responsibility. This sounds much easier than it is. To truly take 100% responsibility for ourselves, we must be self-aware. We need to understand our motivations, our feelings, and how they impact our behavior. Without this awareness, we end up blaming others for our mistakes or misattribute feelings that we're not willing or aware enough to own.

So part of *expanding* into our strengths is developing and enriching our relationship with ourselves. Valuing and accepting who we are. Being interested enough to get to know who we are. Challenging ourselves to be both accepting of who we are and to dedicate ourselves to being our very best selves.

That's what taking 100% responsibility for ourselves can help us do. It calls us to become the best possible version of ourselves—to step up and offer who we are to the world and to take responsibility for ourselves in relationships, offering ourselves compassion when needed, so we don't badger our partners into agreeing with us or seeing our point of view. In this way, we increase our power in the dimension of relationships.

Taking 100% responsibility for ourselves also creates more power along the boundaries dimension. When we can take 100% responsibility for ourselves, we underscore the boundary between ourselves and others. It is a challenge sometimes not to take responsibility for those we love, for their feelings and for their decisions. But it is a losing proposition to take responsibility for others (parents, spouses, siblings, children, or friends) when we are not in the driver's seat of decision-making.

It can be crazy-making to accept responsibility for feelings and consequences that arise from decisions we did not make. Staying clear about whose responsibility is whose is critical for our sanity, health, and well-being, and enhances both our felt sense of personal power and the actual amount of power we possess.

Staying clear about our boundaries has implications for our personal energy as well. Vernon Howard, American spiritual teacher, author, and philosopher, writes, "When you are genuinely strong, you neither attack nor defend and so retain your energy." When we unflinchingly take responsibility for our thoughts, feelings, and behaviors, and the consequences that follow, and do not take responsibility that doesn't belong to us, we are freed up to be powerful and strong.

Taking full responsibility for ourselves can also help us take risks. When we are determined to be fully ourselves and to accept with compassion our successes and failures, we can venture out and try things we might otherwise be afraid to try. We can voice our opinions to our partner, our parents, and our community without fear of rejection—because, in the words of one of my clients, "When I'm with myself, I'm good." We don't need the approval or acceptance of everyone else when we're able to provide that for ourselves.

Taking full responsibility for ourselves also inspires others to be their best selves. In the well-known quote by Marianne Williamson from her book, *A Return To Love: Reflections on the Principles of A Course in Miracles*, we read:

> Our deepest fear is not that we are inadequate. Our deepest fear is that we are powerful beyond measure. It is our light, not our darkness that most frightens us. We ask ourselves, Who am I to be brilliant, gorgeous, talented, fabulous? Actually, who

are you not to be? You are a child of God. Your playing small does not serve the world. There is nothing enlightened about shrinking so that other people won't feel insecure around you. We are all meant to shine, as children do. We were born to make manifest the glory of God that is within us. It's not just in some of us; it's in everyone. And as we let our own light shine, we unconsciously give other people permission to do the same. As we are liberated from our own fear, our presence automatically liberates others.

R—Reach Out

Taking full responsibility for ourselves doesn't mean we have to go it on our own. We are actually able to be more fully present to others when we're taking responsibility for ourselves. But it goes beyond that. We need to surround ourselves with people we want to be like. We need to find experts, guides, and mentors that align with our vision and *reach out* to them.

We need to be open with friends about our desire and intent to grow. Maybe we need to put people on notice that we're going to strive to develop our potential and that may mean changes in the current relationship.

Recently, I went to a retreat with a small group of women all desiring to grow their businesses. As it turns out, we can't up-level our businesses without developing ourselves. In becoming more empowered to grow our businesses, we have to confront the barriers that hold us back.

During the course of this retreat, our leader read a quote to us. We all busily wrote it down. It was a good quote. I liked it. But the import of it didn't hit until the next day when someone was struggling with a relationship issue with her husband and I was asked to read this quote aloud.

Suddenly, the impact of these words hit like a two-by-four. Here's the quote: "Never suppress yourself to hold, win, or influence another. When we are unreal, so are our rewards" (Vernon Howard).

There is nothing easy about taking 100% responsibility for ourselves. We need to have people in our lives who will help us be aware, who will call us to accountability for what we're doing and what we're leaving undone, and who will challenge us to be fully ourselves.

This is where having a mentor, a coach, an accountability partner, a mastermind or a therapy group is so important. Even a small group of friends can serve this function for one another if committed to the process. Because, left to ourselves, it is easy to make excuses and to allow our blind spots to go unnoticed and unaddressed.

Many of us would not leave our homes in the morning without first checking the back of our hair with a mirror. We do this because we realize when we look into a mirror, we can't see our back side. If we don't check, we may miss some important information about our back side. Coaches and groups can be our extra mirror, helping us see what we cannot.

Coaches and groups do more than catch our blind spots though. They provide support and camaraderie along the journey. Last year, a friend and colleague met with me once a week to take a course by Brené Brown on the "Gifts of Imperfection." It was an online course through Oprah's OCourse series that took us through the creation of a journal, week by week, as a way of embedding the guideposts for wholehearted living.

We painted with watercolors, used magic markers, placed stickers and bandaids in our journal—all to gain more acceptance of ourselves and the ability to take more risks with our hearts and lives. My friend and I kept each other accountable to the weekly meetings, sharing ideas and heart-felt moments along the way.

We inspired and challenged one another to keep going and to dig deep in our quest for wholehearted living. We challenged old beliefs and embraced our imperfections, allowing us to think more clearly about ourselves and freeing up our personal energy for life and love.

Not only do other people help us stay accountable, motivated, and inspired, research shows that females in particular respond to stress by "tending and befriending" (Taylor). It is good for women to gather in groups, to engage in "troubles talk" (Tannen, 102), and to tend and nurture others. This response to stress also shifts hormones and helps settle the physiological system.

Inherent in this process of *reaching out* is *expanding* our capacity to receive. Depending on our nature and our history, we might be better at giving than receiving. But the flip side of tending and befriending is being tended and befriended.

There is great power in being able to receive love and support. It *expands* our capacity to take risks, helps preserve and increase our personal energy, enhances our relationships, and keeps our emotional system running smoothly. Receiving support can also help us think more clearly, decreasing that scattered phenomenon in our heads.

Up Next . . .

Stay tuned for the recap of all we have covered about nurturing and claiming our power as women. This chapter pulls it all together by reviewing the dimensions of personal power, limiting beliefs that interfere with the development of personal power, three essential skills, and my POWER formula.

Chapter 9:
Pulling It All Together—Time to Get Your Power On!

> *When a woman rises up in glory, her energy is magnetic and her sense of possibility contagious.*
> —Marianne Williamson

So, dear reader, we have just powered through some life-changing material. Let's review what we've learned.

The 7 Dimensions

We discussed the seven dimensions of personal power: *cognitive functioning, emotional functioning, boundaries, personal energy, relationship quality, finances,* and *capacity for taking risks.* We got a glimpse of what it's like to live without well-developed personal power in the life of Sarah, and we talked about what an art it is, really, to be fully ourselves.

Demystifying 5 Beliefs

We identified five widely held beliefs that interfere with our developing and owning our personal power: *Selfishness is bad and hurts those we love, Guilt should be avoided at all costs, Ambition makes us bitchy, Strength means not showing weakness,* and *Self-compassion is self-indulgent.* We added two particularly destructive beliefs: *I can't trust what I know* and *I'm the problem.*

We examined and challenged some of these attitudes around empowerment, selfishness, guilt, and shame. We have seen how these attitudes can enhance or impede our personal empowerment and how shifting our attitudes and learning to tolerate uncomfortable feelings can be the key toward greater freedom.

We have seen how important it is to reach out at every phase of our development and growth. The single best antidote to shame is to expose what we feel ashamed about (this is, of course, the hardest thing to do when we're feeling this way!).

Three Essential Skills

To help move us out of the "wanna be" phase of empowerment, we discussed practical ways we can actually build the foundation we need. We reviewed three essential skills for developing personal power: *the ability to center*—to access what we know, think, feel, and believe; *the ability to ground*—to stay connected to our center even when internal challenges, such as guilt and anxiety, arise, or external challenges, like disagreement from powerful others, occur; and *the ability to develop and use a flexible boundary system*.

Centering—First we looked at the importance of centering ourselves and went through visualization exercises to foster this ability. We identified how important it is to develop and enhance a relationship with ourselves—to get to know, accept, and value what we find inside.

Grounding—If centering is our ability to look inside and know what we think, feel, know and believe, grounding is the way we stay connected to ourselves. Grounding is what helps us hold onto our values, perceptions, and beliefs when we're challenged by internal feelings of doubt, shame, or guilt. Grounding is also what helps us withstand the challenges from others when we bump up against their power or engage with them in disagreements.

The first of two metaphors for grounding we reviewed is the skyscraper model. Rather than building skyscrapers stronger and more rigid, so they can withstand earthquakes, engineers have come to build them in such a way that there is a counterbalance when the ground moves. This way the buildings can withstand the instability of wind and earthquakes without swaying too much or toppling over.

The second metaphor for grounding is that of a tree with strong, deep, or wide roots. The tree is also able to move with the forces of nature; if it were not, it would crack and fall over when hit with a strong wind. The stronger the root system, the more able to withstand the challenges that come its way.

Grounding helps us stay connected to what is real in the world today. Many of us live emotionally as though we're still in high school—with the desire to fit in and belong. We don't realize that we feel a sense of belonging when we decide that we belong. Grounding helps us realize what is present-day and what is leftover from the past.

Grounding exercises—We went through a number of grounding exercises including high power poses, jumping in place, and standing grounding poses, such as mountain pose, and more. We discussed how grounding happens through the eyes, hands, and feet.

We explored how using the breath in rhythm with movement can help to soothe and settle our jangled nerves or can energize and sustain us for the tasks at hand.

Boundaries—We examined the two styles for developing and maintaining boundaries—the border style and the fort style. We looked at some of the difficulties of a rigid border style and how this can create distance and isolation even when we want closeness.

We also saw the challenges of keeping our true selves locked into a fort deep within ourselves. We saw the distinction between doing things that make us feel safe (but actually put us at risk) and doing things that actually create more safety for us in the world.

We went through the "boundaries and bodily cues" exercise twice—the first time with a focus on self-awareness and how it comes through body awareness. The second time, it was about tuning in to our right to establish and maintain boundaries.

Boundaries help us know who we are—where we stop and another begins. They help protect our energy, so we can channel our precious energy into the relationships and tasks that we choose. Without adequate boundaries, we become more like a boat tossed about in the sea, moving whichever way the waves and the wind dictate.

Having good boundaries is really about having choice.

We talked about the repetition compulsion and how our physiological reactions can, at times, demand that we continue in our old patterns. Breaking free from cycles that no longer serve us requires discernment in how to interpret these bodily signals. During some phases of change, we may need to rely on the support and clarity of trusted friends or mentors who can see us through this challenging period.

The POWER Formula

In the last section we explored the POWER formula, identifying strategies and skills to maintain a sense of empowerment.

P = Giving ourselves *permission* to be fully ourselves, to own our strength, to marry our strength with softness, and to be productively selfish. We can give ourselves *permission* to offer self-compassion through kindness (treating ourselves as we would treat a friend), common humanity, (taking our place in the circle of life), and through mindfulness (neither minimizing nor catastrophizing our experiences).

O = Once we give ourselves *permission*, we are free to *observe* where and how we manifest this permission. We can tune in to our inner voice through visualizations and body awareness to *observe* how we manifest empowerment and where it is still challenging for us to be fully ourselves. We can *observe* through journal writing, which helps us track the role that guilt, shame, and insecurity play in our decisions and interactions. Expressive writing can help us process our feelings and actually promote good health and healing.

W = *Wonder* Woman, the icon of empowerment. *Wonder* Woman reminds us that taking high power poses can shift our hormones, decreasing our stress and increasing our confidence. *Wonder* Woman also reminds us to be congruent in our expressions of confidence and power. We can take a strong stance with legs and feet, be expansive with hands on hips, and eyes that say, "I mean business."

E = *Expanding* into our strengths is an extension of this. We *expand* into the outer edges of our bodies, *expanding* the space we take up in the room and in the world. To truly *expand* into our strengths, we need to know what they are. We discussed the StrengthsFinder Profile and the

Kolbe A Index as two potent tools for discovering our strengths and keeping them front and center in our lives.

R = *Reaching out* is the last part of the POWER formula. We *reach out* to friends and loved ones, we *reach out* to mentors and guides, and we *reach out* to our community. We want to surround ourselves with people whose visions align with ours and who can support us in our endeavors.

Journal Junction:
The 7 Dimensions and You, Revisited

At the end of Chapter 2, you spent some time evaluating yourself in terms of the seven dimensions of personal power: *cognitive functioning, emotional functioning, boundaries, personal energy, relationship quality, finances,* and *capacity for taking risks*. For each, you rated yourself on a continuum, where you stood before committing to the guidance of this book.

Once you've spent time journeying towards a more powerful you with this book's guidance, revisit this activity. In your workbook or journal, revisit the seven continuums, each representing a dimension of personal power, and rate yourself again. Compare your ratings of today with those you did previously, before embarking on the journey.

Choose some specific shifts in your personal power to write about. Describe some successful gains you've made. Remember, it's important to focus on what's working—even more so than correcting weaknesses! If you'd like, note an area or two where you'd like to see more personal power and set about it.

The action plan report in the StrengthsFinder Profile can be helpful in developing action steps. However you go about this, do it with an attitude of mindful compassion.

This journey toward greater and greater empowerment is just that—a journey. It is as wonderful as the destination (if there is an actual destination). The journey is our life. Let's make it as great and as fun and as powerful as we can! Here's to us!

Acknowledgments

Thank you to all in my community who contributed, in small or big ways, to the process of bringing this book to life. Thank you to the women who courageously shared their stories with me over the years and helped to form and refine the concepts in this book.

To those who contributed directly to the making of this book, I offer my sincere thanks—Nancy Pile, Chandler Bolt and the SPS community, Shelia Merkel, Emily Rose, Angie Mroczk and Alaina Frederick.

To the people who sparked ideas about writing, prompted me to act before I felt ready, or helped sustain my energy and spirits during the process, I offer my great appreciation—Heather Abraham, Clint Arthur, Margaret Bratt, Ellen Bristol, Zora Carrier, Jeff Goins, Leah Grace and Rivka Kuano and the whole Unstoppable Women community, Christopher Michael, Christian Roberts, Cecilia Skidmore, and my friends at the Real Food Cafe.

To the people who have been part of my journey for a long, long time, and have been instrumental in helping me develop into the woman who could write this book, I extend my deepest gratitude—Kirk Brink, Cal and Linda Dykstra, Hap Frizzell, Kristi Gortsema, David Grevengoed, Gord and Marilyn Grevengoed, Jerry and Delia Jonker, Marlene Reenders Kort, Sheila McCormack, Ken Pargament, John Rierson, Sandra Stoller, Mary VanderGoot, Patti Parkison van Eys, Kathleen Veenstra, John Weiks, and Deb Witteveen.

To my parents, who laid the foundation for all good things to come, who loved me with their whole hearts, and have imbued me with their deepest desires for happiness and wholeness, I offer my heartfelt love and appreciation. And to my husband, who met me in my "wanna be" phase and has journeyed with me through the sometimes stormy passageway into Being, I offer my deepest gratitude and love.

Special thanks goes to Charles Kelley and his development of Radix® Education, a neo-Reichian system of theory and technique that uses the radix, or life force, to shift and inform personal growth. Thanks, too, to the trainers and faculty, Becky Bosch, Dale Cummings, Narelle McKenzie, and Renan Suhl, and to others in the Radix community for the continued refinement of the theory and the development of innovative exercises. This foundation, these exercises, and this way of working have informed my body-centered work over the last two decades.

As a therapist, it is not typical or comfortable for me to tell personal stories. Yet I have been convinced by the writings and stories of powerful women I admire, including Brené Brown, Amy Cuddy, Kristin Neff, Sheryl Sandberg and Oprah, that in telling our stories and being powerful within them, we create an environment for imperfect, vulnerable women to step into their power. It is so often in our vulnerability, we display the best kind of strength.

References

Aligned Entrepreneurs with Darla LeDoux. 2015. alignedentrepreneurs.com.

Branden, Nathaniel. *Honoring the Self: Self-esteem and Personal Transformation*. Los Angeles, CA: J. P. Tarcher, 1985.

Brown, Brené. *Daring Greatly: How the Courage to Be Vulnerable Transforms the Way We Live, Love, Parent, and Lead*. London: Gotham, 2012.

The Gifts of Imperfection: Let Go of Who You Think You're Supposed to Be and Embrace Who You Are. Center City, MN: Hazelden, 2010.

I Thought It Was Just Me (But It Isn't): Making the Journey from "What Will People Think?" to "I Am Enough." New York: Gotham Books, 2008.

"Oprah's LifeClass: The Gifts of Imperfection," online ecourse in 12 lessons, accessed January 2015 to May 2015. www.oprah.com/app/brene-brown-on-demand.html.

Buckingham, Marcus, and Donald, C. O. *Now, Discover Your Strengths*. New York: The Free Press, 2001.

Cuddy, Amy. *Presence: Bringing Your Boldest Self to Your Biggest Challenges*. New York: Little Brown and Company, 2015.

"Your Body Language Shapes Who You Are." TED conference speech, June 2012. 21:02, www.ted.com/talks/amy_cuddy_your_body_language_shapes_who_you_are.

Farhi, Donna. *The Breathing Book: Good Health and Vitality Through Essential Breath Work*. New York: Henry Holt and Company, 1996.

Halifax, Joan. *Being with Dying: Cultivating Compassion and Fearlessness in the Presence of Death*. Boston: Shambala, 2008.

Johnson, Stephen M. *Characterological Transformation: The Hard Work Miracle*. New York: W. W. Norton and Company, 1985.

Kelley, Charles R. *Life Force: The Creative Process in Man and Nature*. Victoria, BC: Trafford Publishing, 2004.

Kolbe, Kathy. *The Conative Connection: Uncovering the Link Between Who You Are and How You Perform*. Reading, MA: Addison-Wesley, 1990.

Powered by Instinct: 5 Rules for Trusting Your Guts. Phoenix, AZ: Monumentus Press, 2003.

Pure Instinct: Business' Untapped Resource. New York: Times Books, Random House, 1993.

Matheson, Richard, "The Enemy Within," *Star Trek: The Original Series*, season 1, episode 5, directed by Leon Penn, aired October 6, 1966 (Los Angeles, CA: Desilu Productions).

McKenzie, Narelle, Nancy Jonker, and John Weiks, "Conveying 'Stay Away' with the Eyes: A Holistic Approach to Boundaries" (unpublished training materials for the Radix® Institute, February 2010), PDF.

McKenzie, Narelle, and Showell, Jacqui. *Living Fully: An Introduction to Radix® Body-Centred Personal Growth Work*. Adelaide, Australia: CentrePrint, 1998.

Neff, Kristin. *Self-Compassion: Stop Beating Yourself Up and Leave Insecurity Behind*. New York: HarperCollins, 2011.

Peebles-Kleiger, Mary Jo. *Beginnings: The Art and Science of Planning Psychotherapy*. New York: Taylor and Francis Group, 2002.

Pennebaker, James, and Evans, John F. *Expressive Writing: Words that Heal.* Enumclaw, WA: Idyll Arbor, 2014.

Pride and Prejudice, directed by Simon Langton, aired September 24, 1995 (London, UK: BBC).

Sandberg, Sheryl. *Lean In: Women, Work, and the Will to Lead.* New York: Alfred A. Knopf, 2013.

Schnarch, David. *Passionate Marriage: Love, Sex, and Intimacy in Emotionally Committed Relationships.* New York: W. W. Norton and Co., 1997.

Tannen, Deborah. *You Just Don't Understand! Women and Men in Conversation.* New York: HarperCollins, 1991.

Taylor, Shelley E. "Tend and Befriend Theory." In *Handbook of Theories of Social Psychology*, edited by Paul Van Lange, Arie Kruglanski, and E. Tory Higgins, 32–49. Thousand Oaks, CA: Sage, 2012.

Weintraub, Pamela. "The Voice of Reason." *Psychology Today*, May 4, 2015. Accessed October 26, 2015. www.psychologytoday.com/articles/201505/the-voice-reason.

Williamson, Marianne. *A Return to Love: Reflections on the Principles of a Course in Miracles*. New York: HarperCollins, 1992.

Yes Man, directed by Peyton Reed (2008; Los Angeles, CA: Warner Bros.).

About the Author

Nancy Jonker, PhD, is a clinical psychologist and impassioned psychotherapist and coach. Her professional career spans twenty-eight years and includes teaching psychology, supervising and conducting groups for therapists, and presenting at conferences held by local, state, and national organizations. Nancy's long-standing passions include body/mind integration, physical/emotional health, and personal power for women.

Nancy grew up as the middle child of six, with two older sisters, two younger sisters, and a younger brother. Growing up with so many girls sensitized her to the multiple challenges females face.

Never satisfied with the status quo, Nancy searched for ways to break out of the mold of her small town. After finishing college, she set off to graduate school in Bowling Green, Ohio where she earned a PhD in clinical psychology. She completed her internship at Michigan State University where she first began her empowerment work with women.

Additional training in neo-Reichian bodywork allowed Nancy to hone her skills in working with the whole person, body and mind, to effect change. Her work is now more efficient and fun as women learn to use their eyes, hands and feet to increase their personal power.

In 2008, Nancy Jonker moved out of a sole proprietorship practice and founded Integrative Healing Centre, LLC where she has offered body-centered, holistic therapy to individuals, couples, and groups.

Nancy has personally used every strategy in this book—not only to write this book—but to build a business, raise two children, recover from marital setbacks, and transform from a "wanna be" powerful woman to a woman exuding competence and strength.

Nancy currently offers retreats and workshops for women interested in growing their personal power, becoming more effective leaders, improving their relationships, or up-leveling their businesses. For more information, go to www.NancyJonker.com/LearnMore.

Nancy's Story of this Book

Writing a book reminds me a little bit of what it's like raising a child. In the beginning, there is a sense of wonder and great possibility. Accompanying this wonder is a fair amount of apprehension about whether you're up to the task.

Then there's the nurturing phase where you pour everything you have into the development of this living thing. It is truly a labor of love.

Then comes the editing stage, while the creative process is still dominant, but there's a little pushback. In the final stages of editing, it's tempting to tweak and refine well into maturity, but the realization dawns that you've done as much as you realistically can and it's time to let go. The book needs to leave the desk and launch into the world. A process to truly celebrate!

This process was brought to life for me by the Self-Publishing School and community. If you harbor a desire to write a book, tell your story, make use of your free time, or have a bigger impact, I invite you to checkout this resource. It may be your pivotal move!

Get the Resources

In addition to the free workbook and audio exercises, you will find a number of resources mentioned in this book like *Self-Publishing School* and *Kolbe Index* on my site's resource page.

Simply scan the below QR code to check them out!

Join the Community

Congratulations on taking your first step!

We would love to hear from you as you put these tips into *action* in your life. Head on over to Facebook and let us know how you Get Your Power *On!*

Facebook.com/DrNancyJonker